THE RETURN OF BILLY THE KID

By Norman Lewis Smith

HOW I WOULD PITCH TO BABE RUTH
by Tom Seaver with Norman Lewis Smith

AMPHIBIAN: THE ADVENTURES OF A PROFESSIONAL DIVER
by Jim Gott with Norman Lewis Smith

THE RETURN OF
BILLY
THE KID

Norman Lewis Smith

COWARD, MCCANN & GEOGHEGAN, INC.
New York

SBN: 698-10834-5

Library of Congress Cataloging in Publication Data
Smith, Norman Lewis.
　　　The return of Billy the Kid.

　　1. Martin, Alfred Manuel, 1928—　　　2. Baseball players—United States—Biography.　I.　Title.
GV865.M35S58　1977　796.357′092′4 [B]　77-7541
ISBN 0-698-10834-5

PRINTED IN THE UNITED STATES OF AMERICA

For Susan

CONTENTS

ACKNOWLEDGMENTS

In addition to the many people in baseball who spoke with me about Billy Martin, including Billy Martin, I have drawn on the work of journalists who have written about him over the years. My particular thanks to the following:

Frank Deford; Roy Blount, Jr.; Ron Fimrite and Robert Creamer, for their articles in *Sports Illustrated*; Al Stump, for his article in *The Saturday Evening Post*; Irv Goodman, Roger Kahn, Ed Linn, Jim Scott, Frank Graham, and Dick Schaap, for their articles in *Sport*; Maury Allen, for his book *Where Have You Gone, Joe DiMaggio?*; Pete Axthelm, of *Newsweek*; Dave Anderson, Joe Durso, Red Smith, Murray Chass, Paul L. Montgomery, Parton Keese, and Arthur Daley, of the New York *Times*; Henry Hecht, Joseph Valerio, Mike Lupica, Hugh Delano, Milt Gross, and Jimmy Cannon, of the New York *Post*; Phil Pepe, Dick Young, Red Foley, Bill Verigan, and Dave Hirshey, of the New York *Daily News*; Sid Hartman, of the Minneapolis *Tribune*; Ed Comerford, of *Newsday*; Randy Galloway and Jim Hawkins, of the *Sporting News*; William Barry Furlong, for his article in *The New York Times Magazine*; Myron Cope, for his article in *Life*; Gaylord Perry and Bob Sudyk, for their book, *Me and the Spitter*; Mickey Mantle, for his books *The Education of a Baseball Player* and *The Quality of Courage*; and Peter Golenbock, for his book *Dynasty: The New York Yankees, 1949–1964*. Finally, a special thank you to my live-in editor, Susan Renner-Smith.

Chapter 1
OLD-TIMERS' DAY

On August 2, 1975, New York City was hot—an oppressive
96 degrees. Yet almost 44,000 fans made a pilgrimage that
day to Shea Stadium, temporary home of the New York
Yankees. Most had not come to watch the disappointing
Yankees of 1975 play the Cleveland Indians. They had
come to see the real Yankees, the Golden Age Yankees of
the 1950s, play in the annual Old-Timers' Day game.

The sweating fans hoped to catch glimpses of their team's
former greatness. Joe DiMaggio, aloof and graceful, strid-
ing after a fly ball. Mickey Mantle swinging from the heels
and slamming a ball into the stands. Phil Rizzuto snapping
up a grounder and whipping it across his body to second.
Hank Bauer, the tough old Marine, charging in on a liner
like he charged the beach at Iwo Jima. Maybe in those
glimpses the fans could recapture the glories of the '50s,
when the Yankees dominated baseball . . . when American power dominated the globe . . . when athletes ate
Wheaties and didn't demand million-dollar contracts . . .
when everyone knew that New York was the greatest city
in the world.

11

As an obliging grounds crew turned its hoses on a cluster of shirtless fans in the left-field stands, the crowd buzzed with electrifying news: one of those players out of the past was returning to the Yankees. "You hear? . . . Virdon got axed, and guess who's the new manager . . . Billy Martin!"

The introductions for the Old-Timers' game were beginning. The roll of Yankee greats was called, and ex-athletes, many of them bald and paunchy, trotted onto the field. *"Whitey Ford . . . Mickey Mantle . . . Joe DiMaggio."* Each hero left the dugout and lined up along the first-base line as his name was called. Middle-aged men cheered their memories while their children in baseball caps screamed at their sides—baseball is the only sport with a heritage so rich each generation can pass it to the next. *"And finally, the new manager of the Yankees—Billy Martin."* A lean, long-torsoed man, grinning boyishly, looking too young for a manager despite his forty-seven years, trotted out to join his fellow Old-Timers. He acknowledged a thunderous standing ovation, almost as loud as The Great DiMaggio had received. The scattered boos—from admirers of fired manager Bill Virdon—were drowned in the applause.

Billy the Kid was back in town. Maybe, just maybe, the cheering fans hoped, he could bring some of the glories of the past back with him.

In a way, it was perfect. Billy was Casey Stengel's pet and protégé, and Casey was the greatest of the Yankee managers. As a player during the '50s, Billy was the proudest Yankee, the most fiercely loyal of them all, the most protective of his teammates. He was the team's spark plug, the leader on the field and off. And, many felt, he was the greatest clutch performer of them all. If you want something hard enough, and believe in yourself hard enough, you can move mountains or baseballs. So it had seemed with Billy Martin, a player who rose far above his average abilities when the situation demanded it, who worked miracles in World Series. He set batting records in the '53 Series and hit .333 over the course of five World Series, 76 points above his lifetime average.

And yet, fans with long memories knew it was ironic that Martin would be the Old-Timer chosen to lead today's Yankees back to the grandeur of yesteryear. In his style he was the most un-Yankee-like of them all. Sure, the '50s Yankees exuded arrogance, but it was the cool arrogance of royalty, not Billy's brash cockiness, rooted in the insecurity of his fatherless, poverty-ridden childhood. The Yankees were supposed to be high-class gentlemen, not ragamuffins like the Brooklyn Dodgers; but Billy was constantly playing the ruffian role, getting into unseemly brawls on the field and off. His explosive temper, his disrespectful conduct toward front-office executives, his publicized night life—all this did not fit with the austere Yankee image cultivated by the club's owners and general manager.

Martin had left the Yankees in disgrace, sent into exile in 1957 after a brawl at the Copacabana night club, an episode which ended up on the front pages of the morning papers. In the five years after his trade, Billy played for six teams, with little success as a player or team leader. Each club executive would count on Billy's fire to ignite his losing team; but each time his cocky attitude only alienated teammates resigned to their fates as losers, and Billy would be traded. As a player Martin could not turn a losing team into a winner.

The Yankees continued their winning ways after trading Martin, capturing seven pennants and three world championships in the next eight years. Then, suddenly, they collapsed.

Some blame the collapse on the Great Harmonica Incident. The team looked to be on the skids late in the season of 1964. Riding on the team bus after another losing effort, infielder Phil Linz started playing his harmonica. *"Mary had a little lamb, little lamb, little lamb/Mary had a little lamb, his fleece was . . ."* Linz played amateurishly and cheerfully. Too cheerfully. Rookie manager Yogi Berra yelled at him to shove the harmonica. Linz paused; Yogi was the manager, but he commanded little respect. After a moment's silence, Linz resumed. *"Mary had a little lamb . . . "* "I told you to shove that harmonica up your ass!" Yogi yelled, as he got out of his seat and came down the aisle. "Here, you do it," Linz suggested, flipping the harmonica to the manager. Yogi swatted it in the air and the harmonica hit Joe Pepitone's knee. Pepitone, the talented and free-spirited first baseman, yelled, "Corpsman, corpsman—I'm injured!" while Berra and Linz screamed at each other.

Players had already been running to General Manager Ralph Houk, telling him that Yogi had lost control of the club. After the Great Harmonica Incident, Houk and the owners decided to fire Yogi. The fact that the team recovered from the slump well enough to win the pennant and take the St. Louis Cardinals to seven games in the World Series before losing did not change their minds. And the next year, under former St. Louis manager Johnny Keane, the Yankees finished sixth.

Blaming Linz's harmonica playing for the decline of the Yankees made as much sense as blaming the decline of American dominance in world affairs on the rise of guitar-playing folk singers in the early '60s, or the decline in the fortunes of New York on the increasing numbers of street musicians in the mid-'60s.

Yankee owners Del Webb and Dan Topping had long before decided to sell the franchise when the right buyer came along. And by the time CBS offered $13 million in November, 1964, the club had fallen into disrepair. The Yankee stars were aging and not being replaced. The farm system had been gutted and was no longer sending up crops of bright prospects.

The dark ages for the Yankees descended at about the

time people saw a civil war in Vietnam rapidly becoming an American war—and New Yorkers realized their glamorous mayor could not handle labor unions, or much of anything else. From the mid-'60s on, the nation, the city, and the Yankees all seemed to be in decline.

The interweaving of the team's, the city's, and the nation's fortunes went beyond the symbolic. "Arrogance of power" was Senator William Fulbright's term for the policies that led the United States astray in foreign policy. That term could be equally applied to the cavalier attitudes of the later Webb-Topping ownership, and the subsequent CBS ownership, which expected the Yankees to win simply because they had always won. The shortsighted ownership policies accelerated the Yankees' decline and the city's loss of faith in itself, for the Yankees had long symbolized the city's greatness. The success of a home team very much affects civic pride. Most political analysts believe that Mayor John Lindsay would not have narrowly won reelection in 1969 had the upstart Mets not won the pennant and the Series and revived New York morale, so battered by rising crime and taxes and poor showings by their American League team.

Martin spent most of the 1960s in near obscurity. In 1960 and 1961 he drifted from the Cincinnati Reds to the Milwaukee Braves to the Minnesota Twins before calling it quits as a player. For the next three years he was a Minnesota scout, a poorly paid position in a baseball organization. Then he coached for the Twins. Finally, in 1968, he was given his first shot at managing. He took over Minnesota's Triple-A farm club in Denver, which had an 8–22 record, and drove the team to win 65 of its final 115 games.

What Billy Martin could not do as a player he could do as a manager—turn a losing team into a winner. The next year, as Minnesota manager, he took the team from seventh place to first in the Western Division. He led the Detroit Tigers from fourth to second in 1971, then first in

1972. He spurred the Texas Rangers from last to second in 1974. In each case he was fired within the year. The charge was that Martin might be able to manage a team but he could not manage himself. His constant explosions of temper, usually directed at his front office, had not helped his job security.

Now, eighteen years, one month and eighteen days after his exile from New York, Billy Martin again wore the Yankee pinstripes, his old number 1 on his back again, this time symbolizing his position as manager. The unveiling of the new manager to the press had taken place at a press conference in Shea Stadium before the Old-Timers' game. "We've chosen Billy Martin because of the excitement he will bring, coupled with the Yankee tradition," Yankee president Gabe Paul told a crowd of reporters. Under questioning, he admitted some doubts about the decision. "We knew his background, knew his temperament. We knew his plusses and minuses," Paul said. "If a guy can't learn from the experience of three jobs, then he's not very smart. Billy Martin is smart."

Paul went on to blame Martin's past problems with the executives of his clubs on a poorly defined level of authority. And during their negotiations Paul emphasized to Martin that the hierarchy on the Yankees ranked the manager below the president and the owner. "We wanted to be reasonably sure that he wouldn't make the mistakes he made before," Paul said.

But Martin has been known to explode at his front offices, hasn't he? "I'm not fearful of that," Paul said. "I think we both speak the same language. I don't think I'll mind telling him to go to hell, and I don't think he'll mind telling me to go to hell. And as long as we do it inside a room, everything will be all right. But outside the room, you have to be together."

Looking serious most of the time, but occasionally breaking out in a grin, Martin said, "All my duties now are as manager. The last job I had was altogether different than this one. I was corunner with [Texas general manager] Dan O'Brien and I had to do a lot of other things besides manage the club. Here I'm just the manager. I'll be consulted about my opinion on players and I'm sure they'll listen and honor it. But I don't have the last word.

"I'm very happy, very proud, to be coming back to New York," Billy continued. "Every manager feels very low when he's fired, and every time they fired me in the past, people said it would be the last time I'd ever manage again."

Billy rolled out answers he had given many times to the same questions. Asked about how he would handle his players, he announced, "I like to treat my players as men. If they act like men, they'll be treated like men. But if they act like little boys, they'll get spanked." He also repeated an aphorism he had originated: "I've taken the manager off the pedestal and put the players on it."

Billy's ego showed when asked about his past firings. "I believe, in my heart," he said softly, "that sometimes my popularity in the city I'm in gets too big and the person over me gets a little jealous. As for mistakes I've made, I got mad in Minnesota because I was promised one thing and they didn't keep the promise. In Detroit, I don't think I made a mistake."

When Martin's old buddy Mickey Mantle, on hand for Old-Timers' Day, was asked later for his opinion, he said, "I'm really happy Billy is the new manager of the Yankees. That's where he always belonged."

"It's a true marriage," said Ralph Terry, the former Yankee pitcher. "It was destined to happen sometime, someplace."

The current Yankees agreed with the Old-Timers. Pitcher Pat Dobson was especially pleased with the change in managers. "It's nothing personal against Bill," he said, speaking of Virdon. "I just disagreed with how he handled the game. I'm not the only one here who did. It's just that I was outspoken about it and nobody else was. One player can't get a manager fired. We don't have guys who can hit the ball out of the park, and Virdon kept playing for the big inning. I didn't think we had the talent to play that kind of ball, and I said so."

Dobson was right that it was not his complaints that got Virdon fired. It was George Steinbrenner's. The previous Sunday, Steinbrenner, principal owner of the Yankees, sat squirming in the club box, watching his team being held scoreless in both games of a doubleheader against the Red Sox. Steinbrenner, a burly Midwestern shipping magnate and former football coach, had been one of the fish caught by the Watergate investigations. When he was convicted and fined for illegal corporate contributions to Nixon's campaign, baseball commissioner Bowie Kuhn suspended Steinbrenner from participating in Yankee affairs for two years. So Steinbrenner was at the doubleheader officially only as a spectator. But he could no more be suspended from giving orders than a politician could be suspended from thinking political thoughts.

This Sunday afternoon, Steinbrenner was fed up. He and his Cleveland partners had bought the Yankees from CBS in early 1973, and Steinbrenner wanted a champion. Unlike CBS, he was willing to make drastic changes and to spend big money to get what he wanted. After the 1974 season, when the Yankees finished only one game behind the Eastern Division champion Baltimore Orioles, Steinbrenner's Yankees went all out with their pocketbook. The club signed Catfish Hunter, the top pitcher in the American League, to a $3.5-million, five-year contract. That deal made the Yankees favorites to win their division in 1975. So what were they doing allowing the Red Sox to run away with the championship?

Bill Virdon had to go. Not at the end of the season—now. The man Steinbrenner decided should be the next Yankee manager was available now; Billy Martin had just been fired by the Texas Rangers. The Yankee owner wanted Martin because Billy was a winner. He knew Martin's record for blowing up at his bosses. He knew that almost every other owner would rather hire a manager with a losing record on the field and a good record in getting along with the front office. But George Steinbrenner was tough enough and sure enough of himself to figure he could tame Billy. Steinbrenner told Yankee president Gabe Paul to sign Martin up.

Billy had been fired the previous Monday, and Paul was unable to reach him at his Arlington, Texas, home. Working the telephone all day Monday, Paul found out Billy had taken his wife and son on a fishing trip somewhere in Colorado. "Colorado is a big state with a lot of mountains and streams," Paul said. "I finally found him near Denver." Paul flew to Denver. "We talked a lot Wednesday afternoon," Paul continued, "and again at breakfast the next morning. Nothing much happened, but after I got back to New York on Friday afternoon, he telephoned me around five o'clock and said he'd sign."

After Friday night's game with Cleveland, Paul called Virdon into his office and gave him the bad news. "He is a fine gentleman," Paul said of Virdon, "and he took it like the gentleman he is."

At one-thirty Saturday morning Martin signed a one-year contract, to become the Yankees' twentieth manager, for about $75,000. The great Yankee eras have been identified with the managers as well as with their superstars: the Murderers' Row Yankees of Babe Ruth's time was Miller Huggins's team; Joe McCarthy was the manager in the Joe DiMaggio era; Casey Stengel, whose Yankee career stretched from 1949 to 1960, had his superstar in Mickey Mantle; Ralph Houk played out the string, managing the next three Yankee championships, including the Roger Maris one of 1961, but Houk blew his chance at joining the great names in Yankee managerial history by managing eight Yankee teams that were also-rans. Now Billy Martin was to have his crack at immortality. The team he inherited included no Ruth, DiMaggio, Mantle, or Maris. And one of the Yankee stars already had a bad relationship with the new manager.

Elliott Maddox's phone rang early Saturday morning. Until a knee injury put him on the sidelines six weeks before, Maddox had performed brilliantly in center field for the Yankees. "Hello, Elliott," said a familiar voice, "this is Billy Martin. Maybe you've heard—I'm the new Yankee manager."

"Yeah," Maddox conceded, "I heard." He was not happy.

Maddox had played for Martin during the Rangers' spring training of 1974. After Martin discarded him before the start of the season, selling him to the Yankees, Maddox became the Yankee center fielder and one of the brightest stars in the league. Then Elliott sounded off to the press about his low opinion of Martin—and in 1975, Maddox found himself ducking beanballs from Ranger pitchers.

In the Yankee clubhouse on Saturday the two men met. Martin extended his hand and Elliott shook it. They chatted briefly about Elliott's knee; then Martin suggested, "We'll have a talk, huh?" Maddox nodded agreement, and later they had a private meeting in the new manager's office. Afterward, Martin was at his most gracious, explaining the situation to reporters. "I didn't think he could hit in the big leagues," Martin said. "He proved me wrong. He told me he wants he same thing I want—to win. That's enough for me. We both want to win. Before, he was on the other side. Now, we're both on the same side. I feel it's all over, everything that happened before. He feels the same way."

"I imagine things can be worked out," Maddox said.

Martin's first game as Yankee manager seemed to demonstrate that Billy could work his way with his new players. After the Yankee Old-Timers beat the Cleveland Old-Timers 2–0, the 1975 Yankees took the field. When pull-hitter Boog Powell came up for Cleveland in the first inning, with two out and a man on first, Martin popped up on the dugout steps and waved shortstop Fred Stanley to the right-field side of second base. Bill Virdon, a much more conservative manager, had not gone in for such radical moves. Obligingly, Powell grounded out to second to end the inning.

For the first five innings of scoreless ball Martin paced back and forth in the dugout. He seemed tense, and he was; for Billy Martin is always tense. The inner furies that drive him rarely let up. He was anxious to win his first game as Yankee manager. He is always anxious to win, in first games or last games, pennant-race games or meaningless games. He has a driving need to win, and confidence that he can win, anytime, anyplace. Sensing the new mood, the players on the bench tried to appear more animated and involved in the game than they had under the more relaxed Virdon.

In the top of the sixth Cleveland broke the scoreless tie with two singles and a home run off pitcher Pat Dobson. After a base on balls and another single Martin walked to the mound, right hand stuck in his back pocket, just like Casey Stengel used to do. With the Yankees now behind, the fans were a little more critical. More boos could be heard for the new manager. The relief pitcher Martin called for was Sparky Lyle, who had been languishing in Bill Virdon's doghouse in recent weeks. Lyle picked the runner off first to end the inning.

With the Yankees behind 3–0 Roy White led off the bottom of the sixth. White had played in the Yankee farm system during the final two pennant years, and he knew what Old-Time Yankees were supposed to do: he hit a home run.

Later in the inning Billy's first pinch hitter, Ed Herrman, did exactly what his manager wanted: he drove in a run with a single.

In the eighth the Yankees continued their transformation into a Billy Martin team—running, clutch-hitting, fire-eating. With runners on first and second and Graig Nettles up, a conservative manager would have had Nettles bunting, to move the tying run to third and the go-ahead run to second with only one out. Martin did not give the bunt sign, and Nettles singled in one run. Chris Chambliss then singled in the go-ahead run. Rich Coggins came to bat, and Martin signaled for a hit-and-run play. Coggins missed the sign and took the pitch, and Nettles was caught coming into third on a close play.

Graig Nettles had played under Martin at Denver and at Minnesota. He knew Martin's style, and he came up arguing the call. The umpire thumbed Nettles out of the game, and Martin stormed out of the dugout to argue for his player. After the game, which ended in a 5–3 Yankee victory, Martin wryly explained, "The umpire said Nettles grabbed his leg while he was getting up. I asked him how else he expected my player to get up quick and argue."

"It might be a coincidence," Nettles said, innocently, "but the last time I was thrown out of a game was right after Billy took over managing when I was playing at Denver."

Asked about Coggins's missing the signal, Martin seemed very forgiving. "That's a human part of the game," he said. "I don't fault him. The signs are new; everything's new." Billy has always been known for his loyalty to his players—arguing with umpires on their behalf, defending them to newspapermen. He had also been known for being tough on them behind closed doors.

"Can you catch Boston, Billy?" a reporter asked.

"I didn't come here to lose," Martin snapped.

No one thought he had come to New York for the explicit purpose of losing. There were skeptics, though. Dave An-

derson, sports columnist for the New York *Times*, quoted
Gabe Paul's statement that Martin would bring excitement, then added, "It also would have been exciting for
Chase Manhattan Bank to have hired Willie Sutton as a
bank guard, at least until he robbed the bank. Sooner or
later, Billy Martin will rob the bank. He has everywhere
else. Until then, like Willie Sutton as a bank guard, Billy
Martin will be a manager to watch, and a manager to be
watched."

Chapter 2
FATHERS AND CHILDREN

Late in the '75 season, with the Yankees battling the Orioles for second place, Billy Martin sat in his cramped Shea Stadium office, waiting for a night game to begin. He was in a scholarly mood, peering over the half spectacles he occasionally wears and puffing on a Sherlock Holmesian curved pipe. He chatted about history, his favorite subject outside of baseball, quizzing reporters on little-known facts of Civil War and American Indian history.

The talk drifted to the coming Bicentennial year, and to the rebuilding of historic Yankee Stadium. "That ought to be something," he said. "It will be the Bicentennial and the Yankees will go back to Yankee Stadium, too. The other night I left Shea and drove past the Stadium just to get a look at how it was coming. When they tore it down, I got a piece of it—two wooden steps that used to lead to the old Yankee locker room when it was on the third-base side. Some day I'll build it into my bar at home."

The talk shifted to current matters. "The team hasn't been hitting that well," Billy said. "I've got a lot of things

I'd like to try, but it's the wrong time of year. You know, spring training is so important for getting your ideas across. You've got the guys there for six weeks."

The relationship between a manager and his players is often a difficult one that takes time to establish. A "manager" sounds more like a corporate-level administrator than a "coach." In fact, though, a baseball manager has to be closer to his players and spend more time with them than does a football, basketball, or hockey coach. He even wears the same uniform as his players. And unlike a head football coach, for example, a manager is not protected by a layer of subordinate coaches with nearly total authority in their areas of expertise. And he is not protected by a mastery of strategies which are beyond the ken of his players. One of baseball's attractions is that all its plays can be comprehended by any informed fan. This makes a manager more vulnerable to second-guessing than are coaches of sports in which plays are far more complex or are disguised by constant movement.

A baseball manager has to assert his authority on the personal level. He acts more as father figure to his players than as a distant administrator. His job demands his motivating each player to perform at his best in each game over the course of the longest season in pro sports.

It was too late, by early August, 1975, for Billy Martin to impose his will on the players completely enough to turn the team around. They were already set in their habits when suddenly they had to adjust to a new manager—learn how to react to his personal style, his ways of motivating them, his style of play. The coaching staff, which Billy retained from Virdon, also had to adapt. "It was rough," Dick Howser, the third-base coach, said of the transition from Virdon to Martin. "Billy was such a different type of manager. I had to make adjustments."

Looking back on the season from the perspective of 1976, Martin said, "Last year was chaos. Our clubhouse was a country club. I saw so many things that had to be changed. It was the Peter Principle. I saw all these guys rise to the level of their incompetence. I waited and judged them—the players who were playing just for their own averages, the clubhouse lawyers."

When Martin took over the Yankees, the team's record was 53–51. Under him the club performed only slightly better, 30–26, and finished the year in third place in the Eastern Division, behind Boston and Baltimore. Billy Martin's time, the right historic moment, would not come until the Bicentennial year.

The season ended on a sad note for the Yankees, and especially for Billy. On September 30 Casey Stengel died, at the age of eighty-five. The childless manager of the great Yankee teams of the 1950s had lived to see the Yankee managership pass on to his surrogate son, Billy Martin. Billy served as pallbearer at Casey's funeral. "It was the saddest moment of my life," he said. "I had the utmost respect for the man. For me, it was like losing a father." Remembering his early days in professional baseball with Casey, Billy recalled, "Right off the bat it seemed he was kind of grooming me. Why does a guy take a liking to certain people? I don't know. Maybe he thought I was the type of kid he was."

The focus of Yankee activity shifted to the team's sixty-six-year-old president, Gabe Paul, as soon as the season ended. The quiet man of the triumvirate of Yankee chiefs, Paul is responsible for negotiating the trades and acquisitions of players. He quickly began putting together the type of team Billy Martin could win with.

Paul had served as a general manager for the Cincinnati Reds, Houston Astros, and Cleveland Indians before joining the group of investors Yankee president Michael Burke put together to buy the team from CBS in early 1973. When Burke introduced his partners at a press conference in New

York's 21 Club, he put his arm around the genial-looking Paul and said, "This small contact with the Yankees will be a nice way for Gabe to round out fifty years in baseball before he retires."

Burke should have known better, for Paul has always had a reputation for being a very sharp baseball man. Soon Burke was out and Paul was running the show for George Steinbrenner. The Yankees' principal owner gave Paul the responsibility and the money to acquire the talent the Yankees needed to win.

"It's a very, very important thing, like an eraser on a pencil," Paul said of Steinbrenner's willingness to spend money. "You can take risks and make mistakes and go back again. It's a helluva relaxed feeling to make deals in. You can't do the things we've done without that backing."

Paul had already reshaped the Yankees in his two and a half years before Martin's arrival. But now he shifted into high gear. George Steinbrenner's official suspension was commuted after one year, and then he, Martin, and Paul exchanged views on which Yankees should be put on the trading block and which players should be sought. Then Gabe handled the negotiating. "We make the trades *together*, the three of us," Martin emphasized.

The first major trade announced by Paul in the fall of '75 had Billy Martin's mark on it. Pitcher Pat Dobson, thirty-four years old, was traded for hard-hitting twenty-six-year-old Cleveland outfielder Oscar Gamble. "Dobson was a nice guy," said Martin. "I liked him. But he told me, 'I'm going to pitch every fourth day.'" Martin does not like pitchers telling him when they are going to pitch.

The next trades were made at baseball's winter meetings, held under a warm December sun in Hollywood, Florida. Winter meetings combine the atmosphere of a high-school reunion and a slave market with baseball executives drinking bourbon and discussing swaps of players from other ballparks' greener grasses. On December 11 the Yankees announced two deals that fundamentally altered their team. They sent Bobby Bonds to the California Angels for the league's top base-stealer, outfielder Mickey Rivers, and for the 16-game-winning pitcher Ed Figueroa. An hour later they announced that in exchange for Doc Medich, a mainstay of the Yankees' pitching staff, they had acquired from the Pittsburgh Pirates Willie Randolph, a second-base prospect with only 30 games of major-league experience; Dock Ellis, a pitcher with an erratic record; plus pitcher Ken Brett.

Paul later explained his reasoning for the trades. "With Rivers and Randolph we have speed," he said. "Not just stolen bases, but the apprehension of it by the other team. Speed is a real necessity, especially with Billy as the manager. Usually you tailor a manager to a team. But this was an attempt to tailor a team to a manager."

Power rather than speed had been the hallmark of the great Yankee teams. Martin wanted to break that tradition. He preferred to force the action by running rather than waiting around for a home run. Another untraditional aspect of Paul's trades was his willingness to acquire players with reputations for being other than the All-American boy: Rivers was moody; Gamble, who sported the biggest Afro in baseball, had apparently disenchanted the Cleveland management; Ellis had a reputation as a troublemaker. "I believe there's no substitute for talent," Paul explained. "It's the manager's job to handle talent. I'd rather have a louse who hits three hundred than a nice guy who hits two hundred."

Martin, long ago tagged a troublemaker himself, put little store in a player's reputation. When he was told Dock Ellis had expressed the desire to come to New York to play for him, Martin urged his acquisition. By late in the '76 season, Martin was saying of Ellis, "I found him to be just the opposite from what I'd heard. He's a very gutsy guy, and he has Yankee pride."

The winter meetings reshaped the Yankees, but they did not end the changes Paul would engineer. Ken Brett, acquired from the Pirates, didn't find his way into the pitching rotation, and in May he and Rich Coggins were traded to the Chicago White Sox for Carlos May. May would serve as left-handed designated hitter, replacing the injured Ron Blomberg. The Yankees made a $1.5-million deal to purchase star pitcher Vida Blue from Oakland in June, but that deal was voided by Commissioner Bowie Kuhn. At the same time, the Yankees obtained pitchers Ken Holtzman, Grant Jackson, and Doyle Alexander, along with reserve catcher Elrod Hendricks, from Baltimore for pitchers Rudy May, Tippy Martínez, and Dave Pagan and reserve catcher Rick Dempsey. Some minor leaguers were also exchanged in the deal.

By the end of the '76 season, half of the team was composed of players who were not Yankees in 1975. The only regular players who had come up through the Yankee farm system were Thurman Munson and Roy White, and the only Yankees who had played for the team before Gabe Paul's presidency were those two plus Graig Nettles, Sparky Lyle, and Fred Stanley.

Many traditionalists sniffed that all these trades and purchases were ungentlemanly and un-Yankee-like. The Yankees were not supposed to covet other teams' players. The great Yankee teams of the '30s, '40s, and '50s had consisted of players carefully groomed in the Yankee farm system. The "purists" tended to overlook the fact that the Yankees had bought Babe Ruth for cash before baseball farm systems were developed, and such key heroes of the '50s and early '60s as Bob Turley, Don Larsen, and Roger Maris had been acquired in trades.

In any case, Steinbrenner had little choice. The farm system had suffered from too many years of drought to expect any quick results. And if Gabe Paul could outtrade rival baseball executives, well, that was part of the game. If the

Yankees were willing to spend more money than other clubs to purchase players, that was part of the game, too. Owners have always been interested in profits; it's just that not many of them have been willing to invest substantial amounts of money in potentially profit-making players.

During the winter meetings, while baseball flesh was being peddled, Martin was constantly at the center of groups of reporters. They wanted to know his reactions to the trades and his plans for the coming season. There were other questions, too—embarrassing questions that the sportswriters were reluctant to ask but that they had been told by their editors to get quotes on.

On November 16 Martin's twenty-three-year-old daughter by his first marriage, Kelly Ann, was arrested at Barranquilla International Airport in Colombia, as she was about to board a plane for Miami. A pound of cocaine was discovered hidden in a bag strapped to her thighs with elastic bands. Kelly Ann, a redhead who resembles her father, worked as a secretary in Albany, California, and was in Colombia on vacation. She explained to the Colombian police that she had no idea she was carrying cocaine. She claimed an American named John Collins, whom she had met on the beach, had given her what he said was hard-to-get medicine and had asked her to deliver it to a sick relative in Miami. She had strapped it to her legs, she said, not to hide it but simply to keep it from being stolen.

The Colombian authorities did not believe her story. When she was allowed to speak with newsmen, she pleaded, "Please call Daddy and tell him I need his help.

"Someone just put that thing on me," she said. "They are trying to extort me. I think they also intended to rape me. I don't want any scandal. I only want Daddy to come."

The chief of Colombia's secret police also appealed to Billy Martin to come to Colombia and try to talk his daughter into cooperating with the authorities. When asked about the situation, Martin claimed he was already doing his best to get Kelly Ann out of jail, and he complained that all the publicity wouldn't help things. "All I know is, some lawyer down there is trying to fleece me for an awful lot of money," Billy said.

Eventually Martin contacted a Colombian who had played major-league baseball, Tony Pachecho, and hired a lawyer through him. Kelly Ann Martin was convicted and sentenced to three years in prison.

Billy Martin did not know his daughter very well. He had seen little of her since she was an infant and her mother left him, in 1953, after a marriage of three years.

In the 1976 *Yankee Yearbook* Martin listed, under personal data: CHILDREN: BILLY JOE (*11*). No mention of Kelly Ann.

Billy Martin's father deserted him when he was eight months old.

Billy was born on May 16, 1928, at his home in the poor section of West Berkeley, California, near San Francisco Bay. According to his mother, a small, animated woman, Billy was a month overdue. "I thought I'd never have him," she said. "If I hadn't fallen into the coal bin, I don't think I'd have had him yet. I was hanging up clothes, and I tripped and fell and got all bruised up. The next day, I had Billy."

The baby was christened Alfred Manuel Martin, Alfred being his father's name. Billy's mother, who still lives in the same house where Billy was born, the oldest in town, was the daughter of an Italian fisherman and a woman who immigrated to America to marry him. When Billy's mother was sixteen, she married a man named Pesano and had a son, Frank. "Then I married Martin," she recounted. "Let's face it, we didn't get along. He left me."

Billy's father was a Portuguese farm worker from Hawaii, a big man with a reputation as a tough fighter. After Alfred Martin deserted, Billy did not see him for fourteen years. Then his father showed up, bringing Billy a pair of corduroy pants. Billy next saw his father five years later, when Billy made the Oakland Acorns baseball team.

Billy was never known by the name Alfred. He did not even realize he was named Alfred until he attended school. The name "Billy" came from his non-English-speaking grandmother, who called him "Bellis"—short for *bellissimo*, which means "beautiful." When Billy was eighteen months old, his mother married again, this time a Canadian-born Irishman named Jack Downing. Billy retained the name Martin, and he didn't live with his mother and stepfather. He grew up next door with his grandmother. She died in 1946, after singing "O Sole Mio!" on her deathbed.

"My grandmother," Billy recalled with great affection, "she used to bite my hand when I was bad, and when I sneaked in late she'd bang me on the back of my head and make me say my prayers in Italian."

The most influential adults in Billy's early life were female. Perhaps this is why he has such an overly protective attitude toward women. Once, when Billy was about eleven, he was walking down a street with his mother and they passed a group of men on the sidewalk. The men's heads turned and Billy flushed with anger when he heard them whistle at his mother. "I wanted to fight those guys," Billy remembered. His mother sensed that and turned to him, saying, "Listen, Billy, don't you ever forget that I got the best-looking fanny in town."

As a boy Billy always had family around him. In addition to his older half brother, Frank, he had a younger half brother, Jackie, born five years after Billy, and a half sister, Joan, thirteen years younger. The large Italian family also included cousins, aunts, and uncles who lived in the area. Billy would help make wine for the family by tromping barefoot on grapes. And he went duck hunting with his stepfather. He and his cousins and buddies also built rafts and searched the waters for crippled birds which other hunters had injured.

"I can remember being shot at by my own uncle," Billy remembered with a laugh. "See, we used to raid our own fruit trees, and one day my uncle came out shooting. Next day he says, 'I almost got those little bastards yesterday.'"

Despite the support of a large family, Billy's early life was not one that offered a young boy much feeling of security. He grew up in poverty, during the Depression. His stepfather, originally a truck driver, was unemployable, except for an occasional WPA job, because of chronic asthma.

Father Dennis Moore, the priest of the local church, St. Ambrose, remembered Billy Martin as a child. "I first saw him at age eight or nine," he said. "He was a solemn little fellow. Billy would sweep out the church in exchange for food packages for his mother and younger brother. I believe he was able to attend one summer camp as a boy. He scrubbed floors and washed walls at the YMCA to get that trip. The family was very poor.

"When Billy went into professional baseball," Father Moore added, "I prayed he would get some wise counseling. Life had made him most vulnerable."

Billy worked after school and during most of his summers. He was an equipment manager at a local playground, a letter carrier at the post office, a packer for Heinz, and a steel-mill worker. When Billy was working and his stepfather had his WPA job, the family income was about $22 a week.

Unlike many boys from his side of the tracks, Billy never ran into serious trouble with the police. The only stealing he did was grabbing an occasional loaf of fresh bread from a local bakery, and he was never caught. He did, however, have a lot of trouble with his peer group.

Billy's grandmother might have thought he was beautiful, but the neighborhood kids didn't. They taunted him about his large nose—"Big Nose," "Pinocchio," "Banana Nose," they would call him. It was a tough neighborhood where everyone had his share of fights, but Billy was a target more than most because he was short and skinny for his age. "You didn't have much choice about fighting," Billy explained. "All the kids would get in a circle around you and you had to fight the kid who was making fun of you. You had to fight—or run." Billy never ran. He fought for self-respect and for the respect of others. And he developed into a fierce fighter.

Billy found another outlet in sports. "I never felt equal to people," Martin has said of his childhood. "Sports was one way I could even up." When he wasn't in school or earning money, he was at the local playgrounds where he found he could hold his own against much bigger and older boys in pickup games of basketball and baseball.

In school he did not do as well. Socially and academically, Berkeley High School was an ordeal for Billy. He was from the poor section of town and conscious of it. "I never went to a dance," he said. "I didn't have the right clothes."

He was enrolled in a vocational course and his marks were poor. He even received a failing grade in physical education. "How does anybody get an F in phys. ed.?" he complained years later. "I was all-county in both baseball and basketball. You know, the guy who gave me that grade once asked me for tickets to the World Series when I was with the Yankees. And I got them for him. I wanted to show him I could be a better man than he was."

Billy's English teacher was one of the few able to reach him. Realizing that his poor grades stemmed simply from lack of interest, she assigned him a book she guessed he would read. It was *Lou Gehrig, A Quiet Hero,* by Frank Graham. For once, Billy did read a book all the way through and received a good mark, even though he never did attempt to emulate Gehrig's silent brand of heroism.

On the playing field Billy excelled, but even there he did not feel totally secure. He constantly had to prove his worth to himself and to others. "I had an inferiority complex," he explained to a sports reporter six years after high school. "I would look at the other boys who came out for the high-school team and say to myself, 'I'm as good as they are.' But when I got on the field with them, I would say to myself, 'Am I?'

"I was. Sure, I was. I knew, deep down, I was. But I had to prove it to myself and I couldn't let on how I felt. I had to be cocky. All the time I knew I was good, but . . . " Billy shrugged, and grinned. "It sounds a little confused," he admitted.

He played forward on the high-school basketball team, set the school record by averaging 15.6 points per game, and led his team to the county championship three years in a row; and he was also a standout on the football team. He won a basketball scholarship to Santa Clara and didn't accept it, preferring to start his baseball career.

On the high school baseball team he was an aggressive shortstop and a .400-plus batter. Major-league scouts looked the team over and Cincinnati signed up Babe Van Heuit, a slugging outfielder who never made it above the low minors. One possible reason they overlooked Martin was his temper.

Off the field, the teenager regularly got into fights, and he was growing more confident of his fighting ability. He once took on a Golden Gloves winner who he felt had insulted his friend. Billy knocked the amateur boxer out with a right to the jaw. His fighting carried over to the baseball diamond, too. Riding Martin became a favorite pastime among fans in the high-school City League because Billy could always be counted on to react. Once a rival school's rooting section behind third base began getting on him about his nose. Infuriated, Billy pulled an inside pitch into the crowd. Billy's third-base coach had to dodge the liner. Rushing to the plate, he yelled, "Don't be a fool, Billy. You wasted a pitch just to get revenge. You should be taking care of the pitcher."

"He's next," Martin said. On the next pitch he whacked a hot grounder through the pitcher's legs.

Martin was batting .470 when Berkeley met its main rival, Hayward High School. He and the pitcher began exchanging insults. The pitcher threw at him. Martin ducked and headed for the mound—to "complain," as he later explained. The pitcher swung first, connecting with Martin's nose, but Martin landed an uppercut, ending the fight. After the game the head of his high school's athletic department suspended Billy from the team.

"But why?" Billy protested. "He hit me first."

"You should have turned the other cheek," he was told.

"I got kicked off the team, as a disgrace to the school," Billy told Ron Fimrite, of *Sports Illustrated.* He was still bitter about the incident a quarter century later. "If I'd been a different kind of kid, I might be a criminal today."

The team's other star, Babe Van Heuit, recalled, "I've never seen anyone so broken up. Billy would hang around the practice field like a lost soul."

Though high-school baseball did not provide Billy with a shot at professional baseball, sandlot ball did. Billy had started playing in the Berkeley sandlots when he was in his mid-teens, a gawky, five-foot-five, 125-pounder. And the competition was rough, especially during the off-season, when major leaguers, Pacific Coast leaguers, and other professionals would be around looking for a game. At James Kenney Playfield, near Billy's home, he caught the eye of Augie Galan, who had played in the majors for sixteen years. Galan recommended the skinny teenager to Red Adams, the trainer of the Pacific Coast League's Oakland Acorns, a Triple-A club one step below the majors. Adams also managed a junior team that performed before the professional games at the Oakland ballpark. As a member of the junior team, Billy was soon playing skillfully and aggressively enough to convince Adams he had a real discovery on his hands.

The Acorns had a new manager that year—Casey Stengel. Casey's baseball career at that point seemed to be sinking fast. The major-league teams Stengel had managed had been losers, and at fifty-five, he was better known as a clown than as an intelligent baseball man. Adams kept insisting that Casey take a look at his shortstop, Martin, but Casey was not interested. Finally, Adams smuggled Martin into the ballpark for a workout with a number of recently signed players.

"I remember the first time I saw that fresh kid quite well," Casey recalled a few years later. "Red Adams had some of our bonus boys out early this spring day. They were dressed up fit to kill. Then out on the diamond comes this skinny kid. If he hadn't been moving I'd have thought him a scarecrow. He wore his own tattered uniform and a silly-looking cap. Red put him in at shortstop. After practice I told Adams his second baseman looked pretty good. 'No, you're wrong,' Adams told me. 'The best player on the field was the shortstop.' 'You mean that ragamuffin?' I asked. 'Yep, that's the one,' said Red. 'He'll be back tomorrow. Take another look at him.'"

The next day, Casey hit grounders at Billy Martin for an hour. Martin hustled and scrambled, and even when he couldn't make a clean stop, he got in front of the ball. "Casey would glare at me and grit his teeth and cock his head over to one side—and *whack*—he'd drive me a hot one," Martin said. "I'd catch it and give him the limp wrist and throw it back."

"The kid threw a little like a girl but you could see he was a ballplayer," Casey said. "'He's for us,' I told Red. 'I like him.'"

Eddie Leishman, a Yankee scout, was looking for an infielder for the Idaho Falls club in the low minors. Casey recommended Martin to him, so Billy was offered an Oakland contract. Oakland would own him while he was farmed out to Idaho.

"I never thought about a bonus," said Martin, who received one of $300. "All I wanted was to be a ballplayer, and this was my chance."

Martin's reputation had preceded him, and Oakland owner Brick Laws had one request. He asked that Billy break off his ties with the street gang he hung around with. Martin, who wanted to be a ballplayer more than anything else in the world, had his code of honor, however, and it included loyalty to one's friends. "Sir," he said, "if I have to do that, I don't want to play ball for you."

Laws accepted, and Billy became a professional baseball player, to the surprise of many in his neighborhood and his high school.

Chapter 3
A TEENAGER'S WORLD

It was sunny but cool on April 14, 1976, as the New York Yankees took their first batting practice at the "new" Yankee Stadium, remodeled by the city at the cost of $100 million. For two seasons the Yankees had played their home games in the alien environs of Shea Stadium, built for the Mets and the Jets. Only eight of the current Yankees had worn pinstripes in Yankee Stadium. But the current manager had.

As the Yankees practiced before the season's home opener, Martin surveyed the scene. The $100-million renovation had changed many things about Billy's old ballpark. Gone were the columns that used to block the view of the field from some seats. Gone was the majestic copper facade along the upper deck. Gone were the light towers, replaced by more modern lights edging the top rim of the stadium. The dimensions of the playing field had also been altered. The center-field fence was now 430 feet away from home, instead of 457. The seats were wider now, and the bright, shining blue color made the Stadium look brand new instead of fifty-three years old.

Despite the alterations, enough remained the same to make it feel like home to Billy Martin. He carefully checked all the work that had been done. Details are important to Martin—details are what win games. Billy found some problems on the field. He saw that the infield was not perfectly level and that there was a hump in the outfield; the grounds crew was informed. He noticed a narrow slit at the top of the dugout stairs where players could catch their spikes, and exposed pipes a catcher might run into chasing a foul pop. He gave orders to fill in the slit and pad the pipes.

Back in the clubhouse, the manager's office failed to please him. It looked barren, with its white cinderblock walls and bare cement floor. The only pieces of furniture were Martin's desk and two other chairs.

"I need a carpet in my office," the manager demanded. "I need furniture. I need a shower head for my shower." He noted that the players' area was carpeted, but the carpeting ended at his office. "You think they're trying to tell me something?" Billy said, smiling. "It's the same old stuff. Nobody cares about the manager. I think I'll play out my option." Still, Billy was pleased.

He was happy to be back in Yankee Stadium. He was especially happy to be coming home in first place, with a 3–1 record at this early stage in the season. Too early, perhaps, to mean anything in the long run, but it was fitting for the Yankee opener, and every win pleases Martin. Perhaps even more important to Billy, he liked the way his team looked and he liked their attitude.

Ed Figueroa, the new pitcher, wandered into the clubhouse, an hour late for practice. George Steinbrenner had ordered all players to be remodeled for the Yankee Stadium opener—no long or shaggy hair would be permitted. Martin had given Figueroa permission to be late for practice in order to find a barber. Figueroa walked up to Martin and showed him the back of his freshly barbered head. Billy smiled and nodded his approval.

The 1976 Yankees were Billy Martin's team. After the winter trades had reshaped the personnel, Martin took on the job of reshaping their psyches. He was not going to have a "country club" atmosphere this year. Before spring training, he wrote a letter to each member of the team, old and new, telling him what he expected.

Spring training was delayed, and half the exhibition schedule wiped out, by a labor dispute between the Baseball Players Association and the owners. When training finally opened, Martin held a team meeting. He talked of Yankee pride. He evoked the Yankee traditions. "The old Yankees helped each other," he said. He told how Jerry Coleman helped teach him to play second base, even though Martin was after his job.

The Yankees' record was 10–7 in spring training—not sensational, but Billy liked the way they played. "We became a team in spring training," he said later.

Before opening day in Milwaukee, Martin was optimistic. "We didn't have too much time down there," he said, "but the players generally have the idea of what I want. We've been aggressive and sometimes we've been overaggressive or foolishly aggressive. But you have to do that to break away from the other way of doing things. The key to our season is pitching. If the pitching comes through like I think it will, we'll win."

Not everyone shared Martin's confidence. Most sportswriters predicted that the Boston Red Sox would repeat as Eastern Division champions with their main competition coming from the Baltimore Orioles. Before opening day, Dave Anderson, of the *Times*, wrote, "The Yankees might not finish higher than fourth."

New York, behind Catfish Hunter, lost the opening game to the Milwaukee Brewers, 5–0. The next day Milwaukee's Don Money seemed to hit a grand-slam homer—but only "seemed." For it turned out that an umpire had called time-out on Chris Chambliss's request before the pitch, and the home run was called back. The Yankees capitalized on that piece of luck and went on to win that game, and the next two, before their return home.

The reopening day of Yankee Stadium was an occasion for nostalgia, civic pride, and civic anger. Outside the gates, picketers complained about the bankrupt city's spending $100 million on the Stadium while the neighborhood around it, the edge of the South Bronx ghetto, received only broken promises. The fans inside the Stadium, however, were happy. A sellout crowd of 54,010, including many celebrities, politicians, and dignitaries, watched a forty-five-minute salute to the Stadium's past as a home for great sporting events in football and boxing as well as in baseball. Presented to the crowd were Joe Louis and Frank Gifford, Mickey Mantle and Joe DiMaggio, Mrs. Babe Ruth and Mrs. Lou Gehrig, and six members of the 1923 Yankee team which had opened the old Stadium. Former Yankee Bobby Richardson delivered the invocation. As Martin bowed his head and listened intently, the man who had succeeded him as Yankee second baseman prayed for all the people gathered at the Stadium that day.

Martin remembered Bobby Richardson, a brilliant young athlete who had everything the Yankees wanted in a player. When Richardson joined the club, he had more skills than did Martin, then the 29-year-old incumbent at second base. He was quiet and religious, unlike the boisterous Martin, who never let his religion interfere with a good time. Bobby did not hang around nightclubs, or get into fights on the field, or talk back to Yankee front-office executives. He drank milk instead of booze. He was the perfect Yankee, fitting the image the front office tried so hard to cultivate. Billy did not fit that image. Had Richardson not come along, General Manager George Weiss might have swallowed his distaste for Martin a little longer instead of trading him to Kansas City in 1957.

The ceremonies ended, the game began, and the Yankees quickly fell behind. The Minnesota Twins, the first team

Martin had managed in the majors, scored three runs in the first and another in the third. With two outs in the third, Martin came out to the mound to remove pitcher Rudy May. The eyes of 54,010 customers focused on the new Yankee manager as he walked out. Some noticed the black band on his sleeve, worn in memory of Casey Stengel.

A baseball manager is a boss. Like all bosses, in sports or in other businesses, he controls the livelihoods of those who work under him, and his decisions affect the profits and losses of his corporation. But in no other sport, and in few other businesses, is an executive in such a position to attract the attention of thousands. A football coach or basketball coach can call a time-out, but he cannot then walk slowly to the middle of the field to remove a player. He cannot control the drama of a game in the same way a baseball manager can.

Martin called Dick Tidrow in to relieve. After the Twins scored their fourth run, Tidrow shut them out for five innings. Then Martin sent in Sparky Lyle when Tidrow began to tire, and Lyle performed as Martin wished, allowing no more runs.

Meanwhile, the Yankee offense did an imitation of the old Bronx Bombers. They scored one run in the third, four in the fourth and six in the eighth. Oscar Gamble, newly acquired from Cleveland, hit a single, a double, and a triple, driving in three runs. Mickey Rivers, newly acquired from California, had three hits and two RBIs. It was a traditional, old-fashioned Yankee win—coming from behind with overwhelming offense. After the game Martin beamed. "We had to break in the new Stadium right," he said.

The crowd filing out of the Stadium was happy. It was not a typical Yankee crowd. Many were celebrities and rich people, attending a special event rather than a baseball game. But typical baseball fans were there, too—working-class people, families and teenage boys.

Teenage boys always form a major part of a baseball crowd. They acquire their enthusiasm for baseball at an early age. Young boys—and some girls, too—like baseball because they can understand it better than other games. They appreciate the slow pace, if for no other reason than that the game does not demand total concentration at all times. Those who stay with the sport into their teens, before college or careers distract them, become baseball's most dedicated fans. Look around, next time you're at a baseball game. Notice all the teenage boys, there with fathers, there alone. If you want to know a score, or an obscure statistic, ask them; for they know this game of baseball more thoroughly now than they ever will. They are the heart of a baseball crowd.

Billy Martin was scarcely eighteen when he entered the world of baseball, which except for one year he was never to leave. Baseball was a perfect world for him. It was a masculine society, as opposed to the female-dominated family he was leaving. He could be accepted as one of the boys, even as a man among men.

Martin was paid $200 a month to play at Idaho Falls. With part of his $300 bonus for signing, he bought a suitcase and a pair of slacks—luxuries for him. The season was well underway when he arrived. He was immediately put in at third base, replacing an injured starter. In the first inning, with one out and a runner on first, a grounder was hit toward third. Even though Billy saw the ball roll foul, he scooped it up and threw to second to start a double play. Then he trotted off the field, not even glancing at the umpire. Decoyed, perhaps, by the third baseman's actions, the umpire never called the ball foul.

Sophisticated as he was on the field, Billy was still an insecure teenager off the field. Most of the other players were old enough to drink in bars, but Billy wasn't. He was lonely and anxious to succeed in this world of men. Most of the team ate in a small restaurant in town, and like all ballplayers, they tried to make it with the prettiest waitress. Billy had little experience with girls and did not try to compete. One day, though, he learned that it was the waitress's birthday, so he left a dollar tip on the table after breakfast. The waitress called to him, before he left, "Hey, you forgot a dollar."

Billy said, "No, that's for your birthday," and grinned charmingly at her.

The next day, as the team bus was about to pull out for a road trip, the waitress came to the depot. She grabbed Billy, saying, "Here's something for good luck," and kissed him, in front of his teammates. Billy was the target of razzing for the entire trip. He was embarrassed, and he enjoyed it. Unable to convince his teammates that he didn't really have anything going with the waitress, he stopped trying. Billy felt a little more like one of the boys now.

In 32 games with Idaho, Billy Martin hit only .254 and had 16 errors. Nevertheless, he spent spring training of 1947 with the Oakland club. This was the big time to Martin. "On the Coast, the Coast League is the only league. You never see the big leagues and this is the big league to you," Billy recalled a few years later. "I figured, now I am in the biggest league I will ever see and I am fighting myself, telling myself I am as good as the other Oakland players. Not better, maybe, but as good. When the training season is over, I figure I have it made."

Casey Stengel did not figure it that way. He sent Billy to play with Phoenix in the Arizona-Texas League, a step up from Idaho Falls and a couple of steps below the Pacific Coast League. Before catching his train for the Southwest, Martin told Casey, "You sure blew one, Casey."

Casey's strategy was right, however, and by the end of the season Billy knew it. He had a season that finally established his confidence as a ballplayer. He hit .392 with 174

RBIs and led the league's third basemen in putouts and assists. He also led the league in errors, but that was because he went after every ball hit in his vicinity. At a dinner at the end of the season, he was honored as the league's Most Valuable Player and presented with a plaque on which his accomplishments were inscribed. Fighting back the tears of pleasure, Billy accepted the plaque and read it. Then, with outrage in his voice, he piped up, "Hey, someone made a mistake. I didn't hit three-ninety; I hit three-ninety-two!"

Billy learned more than just confidence during his season at Phoenix. His team, under a tough player-manager named Arky Biggs, had a motto—"Knock 'em down." That's how Martin played the game. His already-hard-nosed attitudes were encouraged.

Martin made his mark off the field as well as on it. More assured now that he was a star, he attracted attention as a cutup. The team made its road trips in station wagons, and at one stop, Martin noticed a turkey ranch beside the road. He bounded over the fence, old duck hunter that he was, and grabbed a turkey, intending for his teammates and himself to feast on fresh bird that night.

"I didn't know turkeys were so big and tough," Martin remembered. "I finally got him wrapped up in my uniform and back into the wagon. Biggs was driving, and just before he stepped on the starter, he heard a sound—'*gurble, gurble.*' He turned around and asked, 'What's that?' Nobody said a word. Biggs turned back to start the car and the turkey gurbled again. Biggs turned around and saw this turkey head peaking out of my sleeve and yelled, 'Put him back!' 'But, Arky,' I said, 'he's already scratched me up.' That didn't make any difference to Arky, and back the turkey went."

As Phoenix's season drew to a close, Martin was promoted to Oakland for the last month of the '47 season. Partially because of his eagerness to develop his own younger players on a team of old vets, Casey Stengel took a liking to

Martin. The relationship between the brash youngster and the craggy old manager began to bloom. Casey hit grounders to Billy by the hour, and bragged to the older, lazier players, "That big-nosed kid never gets tired." Casey set out to teach the nineteen-year-old everything he knew about baseball. He liked the boy's eagerness to learn, and he liked his spunky self-confidence.

Casey loved to tell about his teaching Billy how to make the double play at second base. "I asked him how he makes it," Casey said, "and he shows me and I say it's all right. So he says to me, freshlike, 'Show me the way you want me to do it and I'll do it, but I still don't see what's wrong with my way. I got quick hands, and quick feet.'

"I tell him, 'You ain't on the dance floor jitterbugging,' and he says to me, 'Don't knock it cause you can't do it.' Another kid I'd tell to take off his uniform and get out of my sight, but not this kid, because he wants to play so bad it sticks out all over him."

Billy's cockiness, Stengel recognized, came from eagerness to be the best, not from a belief that he was already the best. Martin studied pitchers and batters. He learned that in late innings, when a fastball pitcher is tiring, he should shift his position in the infield, expecting the batter to pull the ball more. He studied the different ways grounders moved on wet and dry grass, high- and low-cut grass.

Casey had his student room with ex-major-leaguer Cookie Lavagetto. "I never knew a young ballplayer so eager to learn," Cookie said. "All he wanted to talk about was baseball. We would get up in the room and he would start asking me questions. I would tell him everything I could think about the games I had played."

Billy appreciated Cookie's advice. "I can't tell you how grateful I am to Casey for rooming me with Lavagetto—or how grateful I am to Cookie for the help he gave me," Billy said after he had made the Yankees. "I'll never forget what he said to me one night. He said, 'There are a lot of fellows in the minor leagues who have the ability to play in the majors, but they will never make it because they have no guts.'"

At the beginning of the 1948 season Casey still had no room for Martin in the starting lineup, and Billy was becoming frustrated. Once, during training camp, Casey hollered, "Martin, get over here." Billy eagerly jumped up, ready to go into the game. "Stick around, kid," Casey said. "I may need you to umpire."

In one game, early in the season, Casey started Martin, then pulled him out for a pinch hitter. Martin approached Casey on the bench and complained, but all Casey would say to him was, "Fresh busher." Casey, however, combined special attention and pats on the head with his hard-boiled attitude toward Martin. Their relationship developed into such a warmth and closeness that in later years Martin would say, "I loved that old man. I loved him like a father. I don't know what I might have been doing today if it were not for him."

Dario Lodigiani, an aging second baseman, was injured in the second month of the season, and Billy took over. He played a spirited second base, and when Lodigiani returned, Billy remained a regular—at second, short, or third.

Inevitably, Martin soon had a fight on the field. And Billy remembered one aspect of the brawl with great pleasure. "Who do you suppose was the first guy out there, swinging and backing me up? Casey." Martin played tough in the infield, and so did the competition. Once, he was spiked badly while making the double play at second. "There was blood all over everything," Martin said. "They got me back in the dressing room, called a doctor from the stands, and gave me a belt of straight whisky. Four big guys held me down and he sewed it up. I didn't holler."

Martin wound up with a respectable .277 average, and, more important, Oakland won its first pennant in twenty-one years. On the basis of that success Casey Stengel was hired to manage the Yankees in 1949.

Martin's manager at Oakland in 1949 was another once-and-future major-league manager, Charlie Dressen. Knowing that Martin was Casey Stengel's pet, Dressen was skeptical about the cocky youngster, but not for long. Two days before the season opened, Martin played a Sunday-morning exhibition game against the Cleveland Indians in Oakland. That afternoon, the Oakland "B" squad, coached by Lavagetto, was scheduled to play a game in Stockton. After the Cleveland game was over, Martin, still in uniform, came up to Dressen and asked for permission to drive to Stockton. "Cookie may need me," Martin explained. From then on, Billy was Charlie's second baseman. "Anybody who wants to play ball that bad belongs on my team," Dressen said.

"Take charge!" Dressen would yell at Billy. "Don't let those other fellows bully you. Talk back to them! Holler at them!"

It didn't take much urging for Dressen to convince Billy to be the team's holler guy. But things did not always go smoothly between the talkative manager and the cocky young player.

In one game Walt Dropo, a giant of a man spending time in the minors between stints with the Boston Red Sox, was playing first base for Sacramento. Billy reached first and took a big lead. The pitcher threw to first, and, trying to keep Martin off the bag while reaching for the ball, Dropo gave Martin a body block. Billy got back safely, though outweighed by at least seventy-five pounds.

In the ninth inning Oakland was leading by one run when Dropo reached first on a single. The next batter hit a sharp grounder to short. The shortstop flipped it to Billy at second for the force, in plenty of time for the double play at first. But instead of throwing the ball to the first baseman, Billy threw it at the oncoming Dropo's head. The ball missed Dropo *and* the first baseman. That put the tying run on first again, and Dressen, though impressed with Martin's spunk, was doing a slow burn in the dugout. The next batter made the final out. By the time Dressen caught up to Martin, he was undressing at his locker.

Dressen told Billy he should never mess up a double play like that, whatever his reasons. Martin, still angry from his confrontation with Dropo, yelled back, "Aw, shut up! What do you know about baseball?" Then he headed into the showers. Charlie, fully dressed, followed him in. With the water pouring over his uniform, Dressen yelled, "If you don't apologize, it'll cost you two hundred dollars." Martin yelled back from under his shower, and Charlie could not quite catch what he said, but he knew it was not an apology.

The next day, Martin walked into the office of the owner, Brick Laws, and counted off twenty ten-dollar bills on his desk. "What's this for?" Laws asked. "I'm paying my fine," Billy said. "Take your money back," Laws said. "We deduct fines from your paycheck."

Later that day, at a team meeting before a game, Martin spoke up. "Can I say something?" he asked. Dressen told him to go ahead. "I'm sorry for what I said to you yesterday."

"Thanks, Billy," Charlie replied. "And you've just saved yourself two hundred dollars."

Charlie Dressen told that story for years afterward. "Gee," he would conclude with a smile, "that Martin was sure a fresh kid."

Though he sometimes played at short that year, Martin led the league's second basemen in putouts as well as in errors, and hit .286 with 92 runs batted in. Late in the season, during a night game at Oakland, a blimp came over the ballpark. It had a band of electric lights which spelled out news events as well as advertisements. Martin heard the crowd roar, and when he looked up, he was astonished to see the message: BILLY MARTIN SOLD TO YANKEES.

Casey Stengel had been eager for his protégé to join him in the majors, but Martin was actually a throw-in on a deal for Jackie Jensen, a California golden boy who had been an All-American football player as well as a star for Oakland. Jensen received a $65,000 bonus for signing. Billy received nothing.

Several years later, while Jensen was playing for the Red Sox, he said of his old teammate, "I admire Billy tremendously. He's held on to his pride under some pretty hard circumstances. Back home, nobody thought he had a chance to go up to the majors—he had so many strikes against him."

Martin himself was not all that eager to make the move. He had just proved himself in what seemed to him to be the big leagues, the teams everyone in California followed. Why should he travel 3,000 miles from home just to prove himself all over again, especially when he found out he would have to take a cut from his $9,000 salary, down to $7,500?

But Casey wanted him, and that outweighed all his fears and his reluctance.

CHAPTER 4
BREAKING IN

Billy Martin sat in the manager's office at Yankee Stadium, his feet propped on his desk, hands folded behind his head, and he talked about leadership. He now had a blue carpet on his floor, but there was nothing executivelike about his office. Six unmatched chairs and a vinyl couch were spread around the room. His white cinderblock walls were barren except for a photo of Casey Stengel, a Pepsi-Cola clock, and a framed sign which read, COMPANY RULES: 1. THE BOSS IS ALWAYS RIGHT. 2. IF THE BOSS IS WRONG, SEE RULE 1. Billy liked the sign, which had been sent to him by a fan.

Martin was speaking about an owner who had asked his team what he could give them to make them win. "You can't buy it. You got to get it instilled here, behind the letters," Billy said, gesturing to his baseball shirt. "It's called pride."

Pride, in Martin's dictionary, comes right after the word "Yankee." "I once asked Vince Lombardi how he managed to instill Yankee Pride in his Green Bay Packers," Billy said. "'Easy,' he told me. 'I grew up in the Bronx.'"

To Billy, pride is the central part of Yankee tradition. It was what he gave to the team as its leader and demanded of them as players. Many of Billy's players had to acquire their sense of Yankee tradition very quickly. For a collection of players who had spent very little time on the field with one another, the 1976 Yankees came together very rapidly. While still becoming accustomed to one another's styles of play, they won fifteen of their first twenty games. It was easy to see that they were a Billy Martin team. They hustled, they ran, they won. And they acted proud.

Many pleased Yankee fans also thought they could discern the outlines of the traditional Yankee greatness. After all, the manager and two of the coaches—Yogi Berra and Elston Howard—were products of the Yankee championship teams.

Like the old team, the '76 Yankees were well groomed, by order of the owner, and they presented a more conservative image than most teams in the league. Instead of sporting some of the gaudy uniforms of their rivals, they still wore the same uniforms the Murderers' Row Yankees had worn—though the tailoring was less baggy and double knit had replaced flannel. Behind the plate, Thurman Munson carried on the succession of great Yankee catchers—from Bill Dickey to Yogi Berra to Elston Howard. Martin even named Munson captain of the team, the first Yankee captain since Lou Gehrig. (When he was a player, Martin complained about not being named Yankee captain, blaming it on the owners' reluctance to part with the extra $500 a year the title conferred.)

In addition, Yankee traditionalists could point to Chris Chambliss at first base as the new embodiment of the Yankee prototype—the modest, dignified, hard-working clutch hitter, à la Lou Gehrig. The Yankees even had a super-fast hitter named Mickey playing in center field, a fine reminder of the old days.

And yet, the 1976 Yankees were not really from the old

mold of great Yankee teams, however much longtime fans
might wish it. Mickey Rivers in center field was fast and he
could hit, but he could not hit home runs. The new Yankees
did not have the power of the Ruth Yankees, the DiMaggio
Yankees, or the Mantle Yankees. They could not sit back
and wait for their lightning to strike. Instead, they used
their speed to move around the bases. Mickey Rivers stole
43 bases in his first year as a Yankee, whereas Mickey
Mantle took 18 years to compile his career total of 153 stol-
en bases.

Centerfielder Mickey Rivers differed from centerfielder
Mickey Mantle in another way. He was black. And this was
a basic change from the Yankee teams of yore.

After Jackie Robinson broke the race barrier in baseball
in 1947, many teams rushed out to tap the new reservoir of
talent. The Yankees, then under General Manager Larry
MacPhail, sent scouts out to the Negro leagues to sign up
the best black talent available. Then George Weiss succeeded MacPhail as GM and made it clear he wanted no blacks
in pinstripes, no matter what the other teams did. Weiss ignored reports from his scouts on such prospects as Willie
Mays, of the Birmingham Black Barons, and most of the
promising black players such as Vic Powers who had already entered the Yankee system were traded away. Only
under pressure from the media and the public did the Yankees promote Elston Howard, the star of the Yankee farm
system, to the big leagues for the 1955 season. Howard remained the lone black on the Yankees until George Weiss
dumped his troublemaking second baseman, Billy Martin,
on Kansas City for a black named Harry "Suitcase" Simpson. Until the 1960s the Yankees moved slowly in acquiring black players.

On the 1976 Bicentennial Yankees one of the batboys,
one of the coaches, and half of the players were black. For
many games Martin had seven black players in his starting
lineup. Around the league Martin has long had a reputa-

tion for maintaining good rapport with black and Latin American players, though he rarely expressed sympathy for the problems of blacks or Latin Americans. When a player or coach complained about being discriminated against, Martin was not likely to agree. "I don't buy that prejudice stuff," he has said. "A lot of guys just use that as an excuse."

Martin does not, however, judge a player by his race. Some managers are always conscious of race; Martin isn't. He speaks of the players who have contributed the most to the team, day to day, and names Thurman Munson, Chris Chambliss, Mickey Rivers, Graig Nettles, Willie Randolph, Roy White, Oscar Gamble, and Lou Piniella. And one knows that Martin's mind is not silently registering: white, black, black, white, black, black, black, white. If you asked him how many blacks were in tonight's lineup, he would probably have to review his lineup and count. Many managers would know that figure automatically.

When Billy Martin saw Willie Randolph in spring training, he saw not a black player but a good second baseman. With only thirty games of major-league experience at Pittsburgh, Randolph was new to the team, new to the league, and officially a rookie. Rookies rarely become starters on contending teams, especially at such a key defensive position as second base. For a decade the Yankees had been searching for a second baseman to replace Bobby Richardson. Until Randolph came along they had found none.

In spring training Randolph looked very good to his manager, who knew what a second baseman should look like. Willie, a quiet and steady twenty-one-year-old from Brooklyn, covered a lot of ground around second. He made the double play pivot without fear of baserunners barreling into him. He hit .292 and ran the bases like a sprinter. Randolph won the James P. Dawson memorial award as the best rookie in the Yankee camp.

On opening day he was the Yankees' starting second

baseman. It is a tough, demanding position for a rookie, but through the early season, Randolph played like an established star. He was rapidly learning how to play various hitters, how to read various pitchers, and how to please his manager. He made only a few mistakes.

Once, after a loss early in the season, Randolph had his tape recorder playing at a moderate level at his locker stall. Martin walked through the clubhouse and heard the music. Martin always demanded a funereal atmosphere in the clubhouse after a losing game. He didn't like any sign that a ballplayer was less than totally upset.

"Pete," he barked at the clubhouse chief, Pete Sheehy, "turn that damn music off." Before Pete could locate the source, Willie clicked his machine off and, perhaps, mentally kicked himself for creating a disturbance with his manager.

Willie need not have worried too much. In his office a few days later Martin singled out Willie as a "proud Yankee." The quiet, talented, and proud young man had cracked the Yankee lineup as a rookie—something Billy Martin had not been able to accomplish twenty-six years before.

Casey Stengel began talking up his boy, Billy Martin, at the end of the '49 season, when the Yankees purchased Martin from Oakland. Stengel won the pennant with the 1949 Yankees, but he did not feel they were fully his team. The lineup was filled with established stars who had played under Stengel's predecessors, Bucky Harris and Joe McCarthy. And Casey, eager to bring up his own players, was delighted to have Billy Martin join the Yankees for the 1950 season.

In the lobby of the St. Petersburg hotel that March, Casey was talking with Billy when he spotted New York *Times* sports columnist Arthur Daley. He walked over to Daley, grabbed his arm, and said, "I want you to meet the

freshest kid which ever played for me." The dignified
sportswriter shook hands with the twenty-one-year-old
Martin.

Billy rarely acted fresh with reporters. Ed Linn, a veteran sports journalist, remembered Billy as being the first
adult ever to call him "sir"—"for which I never forgave
him," Linn added. Billy was not shy with reporters in
spring training, however. He sought them out to tell them
that his name was really Billy, not Alfred, despite the roster listing.

The veteran Yankees were not charmed to meet the new
kid their manager was so high on. Rookies were supposed to
be rarely seen and never heard. As Whitey Ford, also a
rookie that year, explained, "You were supposed to be
around four or five years before you could talk to guys like
DiMaggio and Vic Raschi."

Casey had set up the "fresh kid" role for Billy to play, and
fresh was the way Martin acted. It was a role that suited
his personality and his needs, a good act to mask the in-
securities he felt about competing with major-league ballplayers. "The veterans on the Yankees tried to ride me,"
Billy remembered. "All the other rookies would grin and
act as though they liked it, but I gave it back to them."

Yankee vets at spring training called the rookie "Billy
Stengel" or "teacher's pet." Only later did he acquire the
nickname he liked—"Billy the Kid." One Yankee veteran,
however, did take an immediate liking to the scrawny rookie. After the first day of spring practice, Joe DiMaggio
walked up to him in front of a number of other players, and
said, "Hey kid, let's have dinner together."

"It shook up the whole clubhouse," Martin said. "And me,
too." DiMaggio probably picked Billy out for the special
privilege of dinner because Billy was, like Joe, an Italian
from the Bay Area, in California. They had dinner at an
Italian restaurant. Perhaps the rookie's vulnerability be-
neath his brashness appealed to the austere and self-

assured Yankee Clipper. Whatever the reason, it was the beginning of a friendship.

When his teammates kidded him the next day about the dinner, Billy told them, "Joe knows class when he sees it." As Billy began hanging around with Joe, other Yankees would say he was being DiMaggio's "bobo." Billy didn't see it that way. He told Maury Allen, for his book *Where Have You Gone, Joe DiMaggio?*, "We just got along good. I treated him like an equal. I could kid him."

Martin described to Allen the way DiMaggio walked into the clubhouse: "All eyes would turn toward him. He'd walk by and one guy would say, 'Hi, Joe,' and Joe would say, 'Hi, kid,' and that would continue down the line. 'Hi, Joe.' 'Hi, kid.' Then he would walk over to me and say, 'Hi, Dago,' and I would say to him, 'Hi, kid.'"

Martin also did imitations of DiMaggio, in front of him and behind his back. Billy realized, however, that as a rookie hanging around with one of the game's greatest stars, he had obligations to DiMaggio. "I always felt you had to keep some people away from him," Martin said. "I was always willing to do the things he wanted to do."

The Yankee veterans, somewhat jealous since few of them were close to DiMaggio, could not understand why the great player would pick the brash rookie as a friend. And the Yankee rookies could not understand how a fellow rookie could even dare to speak with DiMaggio.

"I was afraid to talk to him," Ford said. "Billy was a rookie, too, and they talked like old friends. Billy didn't worry about things like that. He wasn't afraid of anybody."

Billy's lack of fear extended to coaches as well as teammates. One day in Florida he felt restless and decided to pitch batting practice. When pitching coach Jim Turner saw who was on the mound, he walked over and told Martin to get back where he belonged. "Who the hell are you?" Billy yelled at Turner. "When you're managing this club, then you can tell me what to do."

After six weeks of spring training Martin had made the team, the world champion New York Yankees. He wasn't surprised. He wanted to make the starting team, but the rookie had little chance of replacing slick-fielding Jerry Coleman at second base.

The team traveled by train from Florida to New York. As the train pulled into New York's Pennsylvania Station, a reporter noticed Billy reading a magazine and asked if he wasn't excited by his first visit to the big city. "No," Billy said, "I saw it in the movies."

He was just as nonchalant, at least outwardly, on his first visit to Yankee Stadium, the majestic edifice which could still awe established major leaguers. Just before the final preseason game, with the Dodgers, a reporter saw him staring up at the stately facade. "Scared?" he asked.

"Hell no," Billy replied. "They still throw the same way up here as they do down there. I'll be all right."

Billy had his chance to prove how all right he was in the Yankees' opening game, against the Red Sox in Boston. Mel Parnell, a 25-game winner the previous year, was pitching, and the Yankees had fallen far behind. Casey sent Martin in to pinch hit with two men on. It was a nervous situation for a rookie, but Billy knew how to handle his nervousness. He hit a line drive against the left-field wall, knocking in both runners. When he came back to the dugout after scoring, DiMaggio greeted him. "Pretty good way to break in, kid," he said.

Billy wasn't through for the day, or even for the inning. The Yankees batted around and Billy came up again that inning, this time with the bases loaded. He singled, driving in another run. Though it is not the kind of record officially kept, Billy Martin is probably the only rookie ever to get two hits in his first inning of play.

The Yankees were loaded with talented players, however, and Martin did not play again for almost a month. He replaced Jerry Coleman late in a game against Cleveland,

and hit a three-run homer. A few more games went by; then he was sent in as a pinch hitter against the St. Louis Browns in the tenth inning. He hit a single to win the game.

The next day, May 14, Casey called Billy into his office and told him he was being sent down to the Yankees' Triple-A farm club, Kansas City. Billy was shocked. He *knew* he had made the team, and he had only worried about when he could break into the starting lineup.

Casey explained that the team had to cut their roster by one player. They were trying to sell their utility infielder, George Stirnweiss, so they didn't want to send him down. "We'll keep you down for three weeks, sell Stirnweiss for twenty-five thousand, and then bring you back." Casey said. Billy, still stunned, said nothing.

"You mad?" Casey asked.

"Sure, I'm mad," said Martin. "I got a right to be mad."

"Then why don't you go see Weiss and tell him," Casey suggested.

Years later, Martin realized that Casey had ulterior motives for suggesting that Billy speak with General Manager George Weiss. "I was a tool between the two of them—Casey and Weiss," Billy said after he had been traded by the Yankees. "When they didn't get along, they used me to get at each other."

Billy behaved just as Casey knew he would with Weiss. "I had to take a cut in salary coming here from Oakland," Billy complained to the general manager. "It's not fair sending me down." Weiss did not like rookies' speaking to him this way. Billy became more and more worked up. With tears in his eyes, he shouted, "I'll make you pay for this. I'll get even."

Billy hit .280 in 29 games at Kansas City, then was recalled to the Yankees in June. He still saw little action, winding up the year having played in only 34 games, with 9 hits in 36 at bats. To occupy himself, Martin would jump up after the Yankee half of an inning, grab a catcher's mitt, and warm up the pitcher as the catcher strapped on his gear. He also learned the art of bench-jockeying. Before a game with Cleveland, Casey came up to Billy and said, "I got a job for you today. Get on Al Rosen. Ride him."

Martin took eagerly to this job and did it well. When the Yankees played a mid-season exhibition game with the Dodgers, Billy spent the evening yelling at Jackie Robinson. "If I was in your league, I'd have your job, Fatso!"

Casey had a frustrated player on his hands, but the "Old Perfessor" knew just how to play on or defuse Billy's tensions. Once, when Martin was ready to explode at Stengel for some slight, Casey walked up to him, chucked him under the chin, and said, "Ith wittle Biwwy mad at naughty ol' Casey?"

"That fresh punk, how I love him," Casey never tired of telling reporters.

In the World Series that year the Yankees beat the Philadelphia Phillies in four straight games, as Billy Martin sat on the bench.

Martin had a busy off-season. In October he married his girl back home, eighteen-year-old Lois Berndt. The Korean War had started that summer and Billy was drafted. At Fort Ord in California, he received a letter from his mother saying it was very rough at home financially. His asthmatic stepfather was still unable to work, and Billy was the sole support of his parents and a younger brother and sister. He showed the letter to his captain and requested that his full paycheck be mailed to his home. The captain was sympathetic and investigated the young private's financial situation. A hearing was held, and Martin was granted a hardship discharge.

Before he left the Army, Martin's temper got him in trouble yet again. Billy and a friend were convicted of beating up a civilian in a traffic dispute and had to pay $2,658 in damages.

When Martin reported to the Yankees in 1951, there was still no room for him in the lineup. Once when a player was injured, Casey finally started Martin in a game. He slotted the second baseman eighth in the batting order. "What is this, a joke?" Martin yelled at the manager. "Next thing, you'll have me batting after the batboy."

"And just where do you think you should be hitting, Mr. Martin?" Casey asked. "Fourth?"

"Why not?" Billy replied.

When Casey sat Martin down again, Billy refused to speak to him. "He's my boy," Casey told a reporter, "but for three days he wouldn't talk to me because I took him out of the lineup. I didn't talk to him, either. But just between you and me, I loved it."

Casey also began to break Martin in as his unofficial apprentice manager. He would sit Martin next to him on the bench and explain why he was making a certain move. And he would have Martin relay instructions to other players.

The most curious instruction Martin ever relayed as a Yankee player was to Andy Carey, a hard-swinging third baseman. Carey was at bat against Boston, with two on and the Yankees two runs behind. Carey swung viciously at a pitch and missed by a foot. Casey called time-out and turned to Martin. "Tell that fella up there to wait for a good pitch and hit a home run." Martin blinked in disbelief. "Go on, tell him," Casey growled.

Martin did as he was told. Red Sox catcher Sammy White, overhearing, said, "You guys got to be kidding." Carey took the next pitch for a ball, then hit a home run.

"You slowed him up pretty good," Casey explained to Martin. "Just like slowing up an overanxious pitcher."

When Martin came to bat, White said, "That's the funniest thing I've ever seen in my life."

"When the Old Man tells us to do something, we do it," said Billy.

Another young player on the 1951 Yankees in whom

Casey Stengel took a special interest was Mickey Mantle. A shy nineteen-year-old country boy, Mantle had one of the biggest buildups ever received by a rookie, but he was impressed with Martin at their first meeting. As Mickey remembers it, Martin was telling coach Frank Crosetti, a former Yankee great at shortstop, the proper way to make a double play.

Billy and Mickey quickly became friends. Martin was then rooming with Phil Rizzuto, who had been the league's Most Valuable Player in 1950. Since Phil was in constant demand, with messages pouring in, Billy began to feel like Phil's telephone operator and secretary. He and Mantle asked to be roomed together, and for the next several years they were inseparable buddies.

Martin played in only 51 games in 1951, hitting .259. He appeared just once in the World Series against the Giants, as a pinch runner, and scored one run. The Yankees won the Series in six games. After the last game, Joe DiMaggio, who had slumped to .263 for the season and .261 in the Series, decided to retire. When he cleaned out his locker, which Martin took over the following year, he gave Billy his last bat, his last pair of spikes, and a couple of his jerseys, all of which Martin still keeps in his home.

Billy reported to Florida for spring training in 1952 hardly able to wait for the season to begin. Jerry Coleman was headed for the Marines, and Martin was at last scheduled to start at second base. When Joe DiMaggio asked Billy to appear in a film for Joe's new television pregame show, Martin was glad to help his pal. Joe wanted Billy to demonstrate the proper way to slide, so Billy put his heart into it.

And he broke his ankle.

Chapter 5
A GOOD RIGHT HOOK

To be successful, a manager must shape the personality of a team in his own image. And the 1976 Yankees were soon shaped into Billy Martin's image. The baseball world sees Martin as an aggressive strategist, a winner—and a two-fisted brawler.

When the American League champion Boston Red Sox came to the Stadium on May 20, Martin placed great importance on the four-game series. "Boston's still the team to beat," he said. New York had a 19–10 record and was in first place over Baltimore by three and a half games. Boston was only 13–16, in last place in the Eastern Division. But everyone knew Boston was loaded with talent, and they seemed sure to make a run at the Yankees soon.

Boston came into the series determined to start showing why they had won the pennant in 1975. Manager Darrell Johnson knew a four-game series with the division leaders was the time to turn his team around.

Yankee Stadium on this Thursday night in spring crackled with the excitement of a late-season pennant race as nearly 30,000 fans showed up for the series opener; before the four games were over, 167,267 would turn out, the highest Yankee four-day attendance since 1947. Boston's Bill Lee, a left hander with a 10–3 career record against the Yankees, faced Ed Figueroa on Thursday night. One of the reasons the Yankees had acquired Figueroa was that their computers rated him the toughest pitcher in the league against the Red Sox.

The match-up behind the plate was as interesting as the one on the mound. Boston's Carlton Fisk and New York's Thurman Munson ranked as the two best catchers in the league. The Yankee catcher had long resented the greater publicity the more photogenic Fisk had received, overshadowing what Munson insisted were his own superior abilities. Thurman always played at his best against the Red Sox. Behind the plate in the third inning of a scoreless pitchers' duel, Thurman whipped a third-strike pitch to Graig Nettles at third; just catching Rick Miller attempting to steal. Charged-up manager Darrell Johnson ran out to argue with the umpire.

In the Yankee half of the inning Martin had his chance to build up some steam when an umpire called Sandy Alomar out for running into his own bunt.

In the bottom of the sixth inning, with the Yankees one run ahead, the tension on both sides exploded. Lou Piniella and Graig Nettles each singled with two out. Otto Velez then hit a line-drive single to right. Piniella charged around third toward home, challenging right fielder Dwight Evans's powerful arm. Realizing that he was beaten by Evans's throw, Lou then lowered his shoulder and plowed into Fisk, who defended his turf with chest and forearms. Down they went, and suddenly they were tumbling around, wrestling with each other.

"I don't know what started it. I was just trying to get out from under him," Lou explained later, innocently.

"It was his kicking that started it," Fisk said. "He was being malicious. After I tagged him, he was kicking at me or at the ball. Then things got carried away."

Yankee and Red Sox players charged from their dugouts. Velez ran back from first, and the usually nonviolent Bill Lee came off the mound to keep Velez away from Fisk. Nettles raced in from third, while Mickey Rivers, the fastest Yankee, closed in on the battle. In a tumble of bodies Nettles tackled Lee with help from behind by Rivers.

As the two bullpens jogged toward the action, side by side ("I was just getting in my running," Sparky Lyle later explained), Nettles rolled Lee in the dirt. "He was whispering sweet nothings in my ear," Lee recalled later, "but it was strictly one-night-stand stuff."

"I was just trying to pull Lee away from Piniella," Nettles said. "We rolled over and I fell on his shoulder. There might have been a couple of punches thrown. I couldn't tell."

Billy Martin rushed into the tumult but threw no punches. His players were taking care of that end. The umpires tried to separate the combatants, by now including most of both teams. Just as the fighting sputtered out, Lee got off the ground and realized that his pitching arm had been damaged. Enraged, he charged at Nettles. Graig, the only Yankee to have played under Martin on three different teams, held his ground and decked Lee with a sharp left hook.

"He had tears in his eyes," Nettles said. "I don't like to hit a man who's crying; but he was coming after me."

That started the brawling again. When the fighters were nearing exhaustion, the umpires imposed order and ejected Nettles and Lee. It was academic in Lee's case. His eye blackened and his shoulder muscles torn, he left the field dangling a limp pitching arm. Lee was sidelined for the next six weeks.

The Red Sox scored eight runs in the final three innings,

with Carl Yastrzemski hitting home runs in the eighth and ninth, to win 8–2. Afterward, Yastrzemski took the long view of the game. "I was very high for this series," he said. "This is a big one for us. I have great respect for Billy Martin. He's a winner. I know the Yankees are going to be tough."

Billy Martin was not happy about the loss. But everyone in the clubhouse knew he wasn't upset to discover he had a team of brawlers playing for him. There were consequences the next day, though. Piniella had a jammed finger and Rivers, for some reason, had a sore toe. "When I came to the park," Martin said, "I found out that neither Rivers nor Piniella could play. We needed an outfielder and I asked Gabe Paul if we could get Kerry Dineen down here from Syracuse right away."

Dineen, who had played a total of seven major-league games, received the emergency call at the Yankees' farm club and was flown to New York, arriving after the game had started. It was a tense, tight game all the way, and this time the sport was strictly baseball. The Red Sox led, 4–2, in the seventh when Thurman Munson hit a two-out, two-run single to tie the game. Boston went ahead by one in the eighth, and in the bottom of the ninth a double by Otto Velez and two sacrifice flies tied it up again. In the tenth Martin sent Dineen in as a pinch runner, then put him in right field for defense. In the twelfth, the score still tied 5–5, Dineen came to bat with two on, and won the game with a single.

On Saturday the Yanks and Red Sox went to extra innings again, with Catfish Hunter winning a three-hit shutout, 1–0, in eleven. The Red Sox ended up with a split of the series by winning Sunday's game, but the Yankees went down playing Martin's way—aggressive, gambling baseball. With New York trailing by two runs in the bottom of the ninth, one out and one on, Roy White hit a long shot to the left-field corner. The runner scored and White headed around second, trying to stretch his hit into a triple. He missed by inches, as third baseman Rico Petrocelli tagged him out. Then Munson ended the game with a pop.

"It took two perfect throws," Petrocelli said after the game. "It was a great play. White forced it. He put the pressure on us. If he's safe, he's on third and we got to bring the infield in and a blooper, an error, anything, ties the game. That's really great baseball. That's really playing aggressive. That's how you win."

Yastrzemski was also impressed. "Billy Martin has taken mediocre ballclubs and made them good," he said. "Now he's taken a good club and made them great. They double steal with two outs. They try to take an extra base in the bottom of the ninth. . . . Six games is a lot to make up against this club."

The next time the Red Sox visited the Stadium they were in fifth place, fifteen games behind the Yankees. Darrell Johnson had been fired. Bill Lee, just recovered from his shoulder injury, pitched and lost the series' opening game. In the locker room afterward, Lee, who had thrown no knockdown pitches, was asked about rumors that he had threatened to retaliate against Nettles and Rivers. He denied it. "Someone else will take care of them," Lee said. "If either one of them ever gets to heaven, God'll probably knock them down with a two-hundred-mile-per-hour fastball.

"All that stuff came out of the Yankee dugout," he continued. "I think they were all anticipating that I would do it. But I didn't, because I won't perpetuate Billy Martin's system. All that violence stuff he preaches is archaic. Time keeps slipping into the future on Martin against his will."

Though Bill Lee might have been overly optimistic about non-violence being the way of the future, he was right that violence was very much a part of Martin's past. Billy made his reputation in baseball as a fighter even before most people began to notice his competence as a second baseman.

Billy Martin, however, did not choose fighting as a way of making his mark. He was driven to it—by others and by his own inner furies.

While Billy Martin waited for his broken ankle to heal during spring training of 1952, he worried. "I couldn't sleep, thinking of all the guys who washed out with bad legs," he said. "I couldn't eat. I vomited everything."

In sixty-two days of restless inactivity his weight dropped from a lean 163 to an emaciated 132. Trainer Gus Mauch, worried about the weight loss, found out from a hotel waiter that Martin had been signing his meal chits, but not touching his food.

"It was rough on the kid," said Casey Stengel. With Jerry Coleman going into the Marines and third baseman Bobby Brown reporting to the Army, Casey was planning to play rookie Gil McDougald at third base and Martin at second. Instead, McDougald opened the season as second baseman. "But you know the kid," Casey continued. "The cast is hardly off his ankle when he is out walking around, and the next thing I know I have to stop him from running."

"Watching McDougald play second base made me heal faster," Martin explained.

After Billy kept insisting he was ready to play, Casey finally started him at second in late May and shifted McDougald to third. Martin channeled his pent-up tension into fiery play on the field, and off it.

In Boston's Fenway Park in June, Red Sox rookie Jimmy Piersall needled Martin while the teams were warming up. Being in a very nervous state himself, perhaps Piersall sensed Martin's thin-skinned vulnerability. After the insults went beyond a point Billy considered proper, he yelled a challenge at Piersall to meet him under the stands. "He surprised me by saying, 'Okay, let's go!'" Martin later recalled.

The two players went into their dugouts and circled back under the stands, to meet behind home plate. Yankee coach Bill Dickey and Red Sox pitcher Ellis Kinder, guessing what was about to happen when they saw the players heading into the dugouts, started after them. Before Dickey could catch Martin, he'd already met Piersall, torn into him and knocked him off his feet. Piersall hopped up again. Martin hit him with a right and Piersall fell to his knees, blood pouring from his mouth. By then Dickey and Kinder had caught up and pulled them apart.

After the game, New York *Mirror* reporter Ben Epstein said to Martin, "I thought you said you weren't a tough guy, yet you run under the stands and punch out Piersall. How do you explain that?"

"I don't like to fight," Martin insisted, "and I don't mind what the other players say to me, so long as they don't get personal."

"Well, what did Piersall say to you that was so personal?" Epstein asked.

"He called me a 'busher,'" Billy said, still steaming from the insult.

Casey Stengel was pleased with his boy. "It should wake my other tigers up," he said. "It's about time they realize they got to fight harder this year. I just hope that some of the kid's fire spreads to some of the others. Another thing—I'll have to ask him to confine the fighting to his opponents. He knocked Dickey's cap off and damned near spiked him trying to get at Piersall again. I don't want to lose any of my coaches."

Two days after the fight, Jimmy Piersall was shipped to Boston's farm team in Birmingham, and Billy had second thoughts. "I sent him to the minors. It's my fault," Billy told a reporter, doubt showing through his cockiness for once. "How could I do something like that? What's the matter with me?"

Jimmy Piersall was hospitalized for a nervous breakdown soon afterward. "I'm ashamed of that," Billy said a few years later. "I didn't know Piersall was on the verge of cracking up. My only excuse is that I was only a jump away from the guys in the white coats myself."

Martin never expressed any regret about the fight he had later that season with Clint Courtney, catcher for the St. Louis Browns. Martin had been anxious to get a crack at Courtney for some time. Clint, a hot-tempered 190-pounder, had played in the same league with Martin when Billy was at Phoenix in 1947. It was a tough league and Courtney was a tough player. More than one of Billy's teammates, including the player-manager Arky Biggs, had been injured by Courtney's sliding.

The Yankees had originally signed Courtney, then traded him away; so whenever St. Louis met the Yankees, Clint played with furious intensity. At a Yankee clubhouse meeting it was decided that someone had to straighten Courtney out. Billy volunteered.

The Browns came to Yankee Stadium for a series in early July. In the second inning of the first game Courtney kicked a double-play ball out of Martin's glove. Martin knew what was coming, but this wasn't the moment for it. It would have looked like poor sportsmanship right then. And it was against Billy's code to start a fight blatantly. In the sixth inning Courtney slid hard into Yogi Berra at home. The time was drawing near.

The opportunity came in the eighth. With two outs Courtney was on first and tried to steal second. Martin took the throw from Yogi in good time. As Courtney barreled into second looking for a collision, Billy slammed the ball into his face, not worried about the fact that Clint wore glasses.

Martin expected an immediate explosion, but Clint seemed stunned. So Billy, maintaining his cool, tossed his glove back to the outfield grass and started for the dugout. He was ready, though, when pitcher Allie Reynolds yelled,

"Duck, Billy!" Martin whirled around to meet Courtney, rushing at him like a bull. Billy beat Clint to the punch and dropped him with a right. Clint bounced up and swung wildly, as Billy held his ground and popped in a couple more punches. By this time umpire Bill Summers had rushed to the scene, along with Reynolds and first baseman Joe Collins; little Phil Rizzuto was moseying over from shortstop to see if he could help. Swinging furiously now, Martin accidentally hit both Reynolds and Summers. Umpire Larry Napp grabbed Martin while Summers got Courtney.

The umpires were of a mind to throw both fighters out, but Stengel, who had quickly jogged from the dugout, argued that Billy had a right to defend himself. Listening to the Old Perfessor, the umpires decided to throw only Courtney out of the game.

Later that season, Martin was asked about his quickness with his fists. "I figure if they can challenge me and get away with it," Martin said, "they can run me out of the league, and I wouldn't blame them."

Martin always maintained that he never fought except in self-defense. But self-defense included for Billy a sense of personal honor and honor for his teammates. "A fellow has to take care of himself; that's my philosophy," he said. "But you have to take care of your friends, too."

"The Bible says you should turn the other cheek," Billy said at another time. "I think about it a lot. I'll turn the other cheek off the field. But God couldn't have known anything about baseball. In baseball you've got to be aggressive."

Martin fought in part because it was expected by his manager and in part because he had grown up having to fight for everything he ever wanted. He also fought because his nerves were constantly near the snapping point.

He played good baseball, too. He helped set a Yankee team record of 199 double plays and became known as one of the finest in the league at making the pivot at second. He never let a sliding runner intimidate him into bungling a throw, and he committed only nine errors in 109 games. Though his batting average was only .267, his hits tended to be timely. His eleventh-inning two-run single against the Athletics clinched the 1952 pennant two days before the season ended.

For two years Billy Martin had sat on the bench during the Series. Now he was starting, against the Brooklyn Dodgers, and it was another chance to prove himself. "I react to what I read in the papers," Billy said years later, "especially at World Series time. I always read that the writers rated the other second baseman over me. When it was Jackie Robinson, they gave it to him without question. I always got the feeling I had to show them, all of them."

Billy did show them in the 1952 Series. He wasn't spectacular at the plate, with 5 hits in 23 at-bats for a .217 average. One of his hits was a home run, though, and he drove in four runs. In the field he really proved his value.

In the fourth game Dodger Andy Pafko was on third with Brooklyn one run behind and pitcher Joe Black at the plate. Martin studied Brooklyn manager Charlie Dressen at the third-base coaching box, trying to see if he could spot the squeeze-bunt sign in the crazy dance Dressen was doing. Maybe, Billy thought, he would use the same sign he had used back in Oakland. But Billy couldn't spot it. Then he glanced at Black. From the expression on Black's face Martin decided the squeeze must be on. He yelled at pitcher Allie Reynolds, who threw a pitchout to Yogi Berra. Pafko was running with the pitch and was trapped fifteen feet from the plate.

Billy's most memorable play, and one of the strangest in World Series history, occurred in the seventh game. The Dodgers, behind 4–2, had the bases loaded in the seventh inning, with two out and Jackie Robinson up. On a 3–2 pitch the three baserunners were going, and Robinson hit a high pop between the mound and the first-base line, an easy play for first baseman Joe Collins. But Collins stood frozen, having totally lost the ball in the sun. Pitcher Bob Kuzava and catcher Berra both stood there, watching Collins, not moving a muscle, as two runners crossed the plate and the third rounded third base. Martin, much farther from the pop than the other three, realized that no one was going to catch it unless he did. He broke for the ball, which was nearing the ground next to the pitcher's mound, and with his glove stuck out in front of him he lunged forward at the last instant. He caught it just above the ground, falling to his knees as he did. The Series was saved as the Yankees held their lead and won the game, 4–2.

In the Yankee management's box General Manager George Weiss had one comment on Martin's catch: "Little show-off," he said.

After the Series Martin was deluged with invitations. He attended luncheons, banquets, and fan dinners, sometimes two a day. He enjoyed his role as the fiery Yankee. Once, sitting next to Ty Cobb at an Old-Timers' banquet in San Francisco, Martin was asked to speak.

"I've got a lot of respect for the old players. But I'll tell you this, Mr. Cobb," Billy said, turning to his dinner partner. "If I'd been playing when you were playing, you'd only have come into second high on me once. After that you wouldn't have had any teeth." Cobb grinned. He appreciated this player out of the old hard-nosed school.

Billy had been away from his Berkeley home and his pregnant wife, Lois, all during the baseball season. Now, in the fall, he was keeping a busy schedule of appearances all over the West Coast. He seemed desperate for the public's attention, as if he feared being forgotten.

Two weeks after Lois gave birth to Kelly Ann, Billy was sleeping late when his wife woke him. "There's a man at the door to see you, Billy," she said.

"Can't you get it?"

"No, he has to see you."

Billy put on a robe and went to the door. A process server handed him divorce papers.

Billy tried to argue Lois out of a divorce. "I fought it out of love, pride, hurt—who knows?" Billy said later. The divorce became final in 1955. Lois's explanation was simple: "I never saw him, even when I was pregnant. You can't stay in love with a newspaper clipping."

Spring training in 1953 should have been a relaxed time for Billy. He suffered no injuries, and he was assured of his job at second base. But he felt tense and unhappy. His wife's actions had hurt him deeply. It was more than that, however. A man driven to prove himself rarely feels happy and relaxed, even when he succeeds. Sometimes the worst period of all can be when he discovers that success is on the outside and doesn't solve the inner tensions.

On the field the 1953 season was the best Billy Martin had in his eleven-year career in the majors. Though his average was only .257, he had 15 home runs and drove in 75 runs, very high figures for someone batting sixth or seventh most of the time. He also set his personal highs in games played (149), hits (151), doubles (24), triples (15), putouts (389), and assists (409).

Off the field Billy was going through the worst year of his life. He still could not accept Lois's insistence on a divorce, and he would call her from his hotel room, often to have her hang up on him. Though he played well, he felt the pressure of the game more than ever before. "The guys who are happy playing ball are those who can adjust to the nuthouse they have to live in," Billy once said. "I've never been able to get a good, steady grip on myself in this racket."

It was reported that Billy began taking sleeping pills. "I was on them almost all season," he said. "Even then, most nights I'd be walking the floor until daylight."

Billy had always been a regular, Sunday-mass Catholic. As he slipped further into depression, he turned more toward religion. He said the rosary in his room at night and began to attend daily mass at St. Patrick's Cathedral when the Yankees were home. Even there he couldn't always find peace. Once, he was halted by a parishioner on the steps of the cathedral. "I know who you are," the man yelled. "If you're a member of this parish, I quit!"

Billy's roommate, Mickey Mantle, stayed a good friend at this time, but Mickey wasn't a psychiatrist. All he could offer was his sympathy and willingness to go out on the town in an effort to distract Billy.

Rival players made the '53 season an especially tough one for Billy physically. Opponents put out extra effort sliding into him at second, trying to break up the double play. "I guess it's my fights that make them hit me harder," he said. "They gave me a reputation and now every guy is trying to make me earn it."

He had another brawl with Clint Courtney. This time, in St. Louis, Courtney came into second with his spikes high against Phil Rizzuto, slashing the shortstop's legs. The whole Yankee team converged on the offender. Martin got in the best blows, knocking Clint's glasses off and bloodying his face. For good measure, outfielder Bob Cerv stomped Courtney's glasses.

In Detroit catcher Matt Batts made a putout tag on Martin's nose, and the two exchanged punches until they were separated. The next day, in the visitors' locker room before the game, Rizzuto complained about letters he had received from some crank who was threatening to shoot him. Martin, half-kidding and half-serious, leaped at the opportunity to protect his teammate and suggested they switch jerseys. In infield practice Billy wore number 10 and Phil wore number 1. The boos cascaded from the Detroit stands at number 1. As the team gathered back in the locker room just prior to the game, Rizzuto said, "Give me back my jersey. I'd rather get shot than booed like this."

Boos were becoming very familiar to Martin. "I was

booed in about every city in the American League," Billy recalled after retiring as a player. "Not just by a few fans, either. It seemed everyone in the park was down on me. Then, after these games were over, I'd get to feeling awfully low, but there was no one to go home to."

"I don't get it," Martin complained during the '53 season. "I don't play dirty or try to hurt anyone. Actually, I want to be friends with everyone. But once I get in a game all I want to do is win. And the harder I play, the more I'm jeered. Sometimes I give them a real tough look when I go to the dugout. You know—under the eyebrows. It makes them jump. I look up at the crowd, and I pity them," he added, attempting to put it all into perspective. It wasn't easy.

In Chicago some fans in box seats responded to an untrue report that Billy's wife was suffering financial hardship. They threw a baby bottle and yelled, "Go home and feed your baby, you cheapskate!"

Some time later, Frank Lane, who had been a general manager for a number of teams, implied that Casey Stengel was to blame for some of the trouble Martin was having. "They've encouraged a jittery kid to play the tough little mug," he said. "You can see why Martin's the Rocky Graziano of baseball. It's colorful and it helps keep the other clubs' spikes honest. But it won't add any years to his playing time. What they should have done, for everybody's sake, was tone him way down."

As the 1953 season drew to a close, Martin's emotional state grew worse. "I was about to crack up mentally before the Series," he once admitted.

A depressed, tense Billy Martin, ready for a nervous breakdown, instead made one of the greatest performances ever seen in a World Series.

Chapter 6
IN THE CLUTCH

Between games of the June 6 doubleheader against Oakland, manager Billy Martin paced the length of the Yankee clubhouse. He was more tense than usual. On that cloudy, wet Sunday, the Yankees had just lost their fourth straight game, 3–2, as pinch runner Sandy Alomar was thrown out trying to steal second in the ninth inning.

The Yankees were still in first place, but Billy was worried. His team led the Eastern Division only because of their explosive start, winning 15 of their first 20 games. Since then, they had won 12 and lost 14. Soon Baltimore or Boston, each playing about .500 ball, would make a move. The Yankees had to snap out of their slump.

Martin tried his best to look calm. "When you're winning, you push. When you're losing, you sit back," he has said. "If I keep my cool, my players will come out of it. They look to you for strength."

The players knew the pressure was on. Now, really for the first time all season, they were being tested, and they had to respond. They had to win the second game.

So far in the season, the Yankees had assimilated their manager's personality in aggressiveness, willingness to hustle, even quickness with their fists. To become champions they had to prove they had assimilated one more dimension of Martin's character—ability to perform in the clutch.

"He choked" is what baseball players say when someone has done poorly under pressure. It implies that the person was overcome with fear. Often this is not the case. The player who "chokes" may be courageous, burning with desire to win, willing to put himself on the line, and unable to translate all that positive energy into the concentration necessary to play well.

Extra adrenaline may be enough to turn a desperate boxer into a tiger, or give a defensive lineman the boost of energy to knock aside the offensive guard. For a baseball player, however, more than adrenaline is needed. Adrenaline does not help a batter judge a curve. Though Martin can define the "Yankee spirit" he evokes as "pride, desire, self-sacrifice," he cannot tell his players precisely how to convert those qualities into the disciplined concentration needed to win games.

One key, though, is self-confidence. This is not enough to enable a player to perform under pressure, but lack of confidence can shatter a player's concentration. And now, called upon to end a four-game losing streak and prove their early-season success was not a fluke, the Yankees had to believe in themselves.

In the second game, under gray clouds, the Yankees went hitless for five innings. Billy walked through the dugout tunnel and into the clubhouse to his office. He grabbed another hat off his rack and walked back out to the dugout. "I ain't superstitious, but . . . " he explained later. He isn't superstitious, but he was willing to try anything, make any symbolic gesture, to change his team's fortunes.

In the eighth the Yankees were scoreless, with one hit,

and down two runs. Billy's lowering spirits were given a lift when Oscar Gamble doubled. Martin sent Lou Piniella in to pinch hit, and Lou drove Gamble in with a single. Now it was the bottom of the ninth, one out, the Yankees behind 2–1, on the verge of losing their fifth straight game, the fifteenth in their last twenty-seven games.

Thurman Munson might not be able to explain it, but he knows how to respond to clutch situations. The day before, the crowd at Yankee Stadium had booed him roundly for a wild throw that led to an Oakland victory. Today he brought the crowd of 47,000 to its feet with a long drive that rolled to the fence in left center. Thurman tore around the bases for a triple.

Now Chris Chambliss stepped up. Chris always tries to relax in a pressure situation, tries simply to see it and feel it as just another routine trip to the plate. And yet he bats even better in the clutch than in routine situations. He did on this day, hitting the first pitch for a single, tying the game. Carlos May, newly acquired from Chicago as a designated hitter, singled off Gene Tenace's glove at first.

Ace relief pitcher Rollie Fingers came in to face Graig Nettles, who looped a hit to the outfield. Chambliss, at second, wasn't sure the ball would drop and hesitated before heading for the plate with the winning run. A perfect throw from right by Claudell Washington caught Chambliss at home. It was the kind of play that can take the steam out of a team that lacks confidence.

Two down, two on, tie score, and Oscar Gamble came up again. "We didn't want to get swept," Gamble said later. "All the way through the second game it was on my mind. It was a game we needed to win."

Oscar bore down; the need to win seemed to make him see the pitch more clearly, judge it better, swing his bat around more precisely without sacrificing power. Oscar hit a home run into the right-field stands.

"We were dragging a bit," Oscar said later. "We needed a

shot of something." He had just given the Yankees that shot.

"It was a big win," Martin said in the clubhouse. "It was a big game for us." He smiled—he always liked winning, but he liked winning in the clutch even more. That was the mark of a champion. Old-time Yankee teams used to win that way, coming from behind in the last of the ninth. And often it had been Billy who supplied the clutch hit, especially in the greatest pressure situation of them all—the World Series.

Billy Martin, in emotional turmoil before the 1953 World Series, was able to concentrate all his nervousness into performance on the field. The greater the pressure on the field, and the worse the turbulence inside him, the better he performed.

Mickey Mantle has said, "There are athletes who are at their best when they are angered, because their anger is always directed at the opponent, or at the obstacle that gets in their way. Billy Martin was like that." Mantle contrasted that attitude with his own: his anger always turned against him and he had to practice mental relaxation for his best performance.

In later years Casey Stengel rated the 1953 Yankees as the best team he ever managed. He singled out four of his players. "We got the best shortstop in Phil Rizzuto," he said, "and the best second baseman in Billy Martin. We got Yogi Berra, the best catcher, and Mickey Mantle, the best center fielder. The outfield is swell and the pitching is tremendous."

In the World Series that autumn, Casey Stengel's best team faced the Brooklyn Dodgers, one of the great baseball teams of all time. Behind the plate they had Roy Campanella, with 142 runs batted in. Duke Snider, one of the best center fielders of his day defensively, had a .336 average and 42 home runs. Carl Furillo, in right field, was the National League batting champion at .344, and had one of the best throwing arms in the game. Gil Hodges was a fine-fielding first baseman and had a .302 average with 31 home runs. In addition, Brooklyn had Jackie Robinson in left field; Bobby Cox, one of the greatest defensive third basemen ever; a great shortstop in Pee Wee Reese; and the National League Rookie of the Year, Junior Gilliam, at second. Most of the pre-Series newspaper match-ups rated the Dodgers over the Yankees at second base. That was an extra incentive for Billy Martin.

In the first inning of the first game at Yankee Stadium, Martin came up with the Yankees leading 1–0 and the bases loaded. He belted a triple over Robinson's head in left, scoring three runs. The Yankees went on to win 9–5.

In the seventh inning of the second game, the Dodgers led 2–1 when Martin came to the plate. One of Billy's batting tricks was to walk up in the batter's box as the pitcher delivered his pitch. The move, though of little practical advantage to the batter, sometimes upset the pitcher as he released the ball. It might have upset Preacher Roe in this case, for Martin hit the pitch for a home run to tie the score. Mickey Mantle provided the winning runs in the eighth with a two-run homer.

The Dodgers won the third game at Ebbets Field. In the fourth game Billy hit another triple. Then, in the ninth inning, with two outs and the Yankees behind 7–2, the bases were loaded when Mantle singled to left, scoring one. Martin, at second, tried to score on the hit, too, but Robinson made a perfect one-bounce peg to Campanella, who slammed a hard tag on Billy's forehead for the final out. Campanella, normally a genial man though a tough competitor, might have been annoyed by Martin's contention he was "plate shy." Billy clenched his fists as he popped off the ground, but, for once, he resisted his impulse to fight.

In the fifth game Martin hit a two-run homer, and the

Yankees won 11–7. The sixth game was a tense one. In the bottom of the ninth, with the score tied 3–3, Billy came up with one out and two on. Mantle was at first base, watching Billy. "He just picked out his pitch and shot it right back through the middle," Mickey said, "and the thing I remember about this hit is that when Billy connected, you could see his eyes sighting right down the bat at the ball." Martin's hit won the game and the Series for the Yankees.

Billy, who never hit above .270 in a full season, hit .500 in the Series. His 12 hits, including a double, two triples and two home runs, set a record for a six-game Series and tied the total Series record. His 23 total bases broke Babe Ruth's record of 19 for a six-game Series. His 8 runs batted in fell only one short of Lou Gehrig's record of 9. (Bobby Richardson later set the Series RBI record with 12 in 1960 and the hit record with 13 in 1964.)

Casey Stengel ungraciously compared his boy's performance in the Series with that of his still-budding superstar, Mantle, who hit only .208. "You tell him to stop trying to kill the ball, and he won't do it," he said of Mickey. "That's the difference. You tell the fresh kid something, and he listens and does it.

"This Series is the worst thing that could have happened to Martin," Casey added. "I ain't going to be able to live with that little son of a bitch next year."

To Casey's regret, he did not have to live with Martin the next year. As one result of all the publicity Billy received in the Series, his local draft board redrafted him despite his hardship discharge from the Army in 1950. He was ordered to report for duty just before spring training of 1954. Martin would miss the entire 1954 season and most of 1955.

Just after the '53 Series ended, Martin was still plagued by nervous tension. With no more challenges to absorb his tensions, Billy went home and spent a week in bed, passing up many opportunities to cash in on his fame. He tried to effect a reconciliation with Lois. When that attempt failed,

Billy joined Mickey Mantle at Mickey's home in Commerce, Oklahoma, ignoring hints from the Yankee front office that Martin should stay away from the team's prized property.

The two friends spent the winter together, hunting and fishing. Eating mashed potatoes and quail for breakfast, Billy gained back his lost weight, ballooning to 182. He also recovered some of his emotional equilibrium before he had to report to the Army.

Without Martin in 1954, the Yankees lost the American League pennant, for the first time in six seasons, to Cleveland. When Martin returned in early September, 1955, his team was in second place to Chicago, with Cleveland still in the pennant race.

Casey was delighted to have Martin return and did everything but slay the fatted calf for his prodigal son. "We need more life and alertness, and you can't live around him without getting both," Casey said. "He's my best clutch hitter and the best double-play man in the league."

Sportswriter Bill Corum wrote, "Until I arrived here in Chicago a few hours ago, I felt that, farfetched as it seemed, the perennial bridesmaids of the American League, the White Sox, might become bride. Now I know better. Because I picked up the paper and the headline said that Billy Martin had rejoined the Yankees. That, of course, just about settled the pennant race in the junior league."

In his first game after a two-year layoff Billy hit a double and a single. Still, the Yankees lagged in second place for another week. A team meeting was held, and Martin took the floor. "I had three cars when I went into the Army," he said, "and now I haven't even got one. I'm broke and you guys are playing as though you're trying to lose. We got to get into the Series!"

Down the stretch, New York played like champions and won the pennant. All the Yankees who had played the full season held the traditional closed meeting to divide up the

World Series shares. Mantle came out of the meeting and reported to Billy that he and the clubhouse boy had each been voted $200. He was kidding. In a highly unusual move the team had voted Billy, who had played in only twenty games, a full share, which turned out to be worth $5,600. "I was happy and proud when I heard about it," Martin said. "It was really something for them to do." Billy deserved it. He batted .300 in the final month of the season and provided the Yankees with the spark they needed and had missed.

It wasn't Billy Martin's fault that the Yankees finally lost to the Brooklyn Dodgers in the 1955 World Series. In the seven games he had 8 hits and a .320 batting average, with 4 RBIs.

In the first game Billy made an aggressive but foolhardy move. He remembered how Roy Campanella had slammed a hard tag on him to end the fourth game of the '53 Series. More important, Jackie Robinson had just stolen home on Yogi Berra. So when Billy reached third, he decided to steal home. Once again, Campy caught Billy sliding in. According to Martin, after tagging him hard on the neck, Campanella said, "I'm sorry. I was three inches off. I wanted your nose."

"I hauled off to bust the big guy," Martin recalled, "but then I thought the better of it. I saw the huge crowd and realized at once I wasn't going to let anything spoil my efforts in the Series."

In the seventh game Johnny Podres shut the Yankees out to give the Dodgers their first World Series championship and Stengel his first Series defeat. Martin came into the Yankee clubhouse crying. He punched the lockers with his fists, cutting them. Then he headed for the trainer's room, where the press wasn't allowed, and he could hide his tears. Still crying, he told Mantle, "We should have won. It isn't right for a man like Casey to lose. It's a shame for a man like that to lose."

Billy had done his best, but he blamed himself for not doing better. "I should have hit late in that last game," he said months later. "Podres had been throwing me change-ups all day. But I should have known he'd throw me fast-balls when the light started getting bad. I didn't think."

Martin held out for a $3,000 raise in his salary, to $20,000, the next spring. Even in those preinflationary times, it was not a very big salary for a player *Sports Illustrated* listed as one of the "four mainstays" of the Yankees, along with Mantle, Berra and Ford. The magazine added, " . . . it is difficult not to conclude that he is the most valuable as well as the damndest Yankee now extant."

Martin's statistics for the 1956 season were, as usual, mediocre. He hit .264, with nine home runs and 49 RBIs. In the Series, once again against the Dodgers, he was again at his best. He compiled a .296 average with 8 hits, including home runs in the first and third games. The fifth game of the Series is remembered as Don Larsen's perfect game. Billy's contribution included a hit and a brief speech to his fellow infielders. Before the ninth inning, Billy called over first baseman Joe Collins, shortstop Gil McDougald, and third baseman Andy Carey, and commanded, "*Nothing* gets through!" The only infield chance that inning was a routine grounder, which Martin fielded smoothly.

After the Dodgers won the sixth game, Martin made a contribution as Stengel's apprentice manager. Left fielder Enos Slaughter had misjudged a line drive in the tenth inning to allow the Dodgers a 1–0 win. Most of the Yankees were frustrated by Slaughter's defensive play, but no one dared to complain to Casey—except Billy. He sat down next to Casey on the team bus and told his manager that Slaughter didn't know how to play left field and Elston Howard did. Also, the Yankees could use more hitting, and Moose Skowron should be playing first, despite Joe Collins's greater experience.

In the seventh game Casey put Elston Howard, who had been sidelined with strep throat, in left field. Howard hit a home run in the fourth inning. Skowron played first base and hit a grand-slam homer as the Yanks won 9–0. In the clubhouse Stengel came up to Martin, saying, "You're a smart little bastard, aren't you!" and hugged him.

It was Billy Martin's last Yankee World Series for two decades.

Chapter 7
BATTLING THE POWERS
THAT BE

The phone in Billy Martin's Minneapolis hotel room rang early on Wednesday morning, June 16. It was George Steinbrenner calling to give Billy the news personally: Gabe Paul had negotiated two huge deals just before the trading deadline at midnight, June 15. The Yankees had purchased superpitcher Vida Blue for $1.5 million from Oakland owner Charles O. Finley, who had also sold two of his other stars, pitcher Rollie Fingers and outfielder Joe Rudi, to Boston for $1 million each. In addition, the Yankees had traded pitchers Rudy May, Tippy Martinez, and Dave Pagan, and catcher Rick Dempsey, to Baltimore for pitchers Ken Holtzman, Doyle Alexander, Grant Jackson, and catcher Elrod Hendricks. George congratulated Billy on all his new players. "Now you can be a pushbutton manager," Steinbrenner suggested.

"I'll let you be the manager," Billy cheerfully replied, "and I'll be the millionaire."

Billy was more than happy with the new players. He chirped with pleasure, especially about Vida Blue, who cost

Martin no Yankee players. He immediately penciled Blue and Holtzman into his pitching rotation, scheduling Blue for Friday night's game against Chicago and Holtzman for Saturday's.

Then Commissioner Bowie Kuhn ordered Blue not to report to the Yankees, and Fingers and Rudi not to report to Boston, until he could conduct a hearing on the propriety of Finley's supersale. On Thursday Martin expressed his annoyance with Kuhn's interference, temporary though he expected it to be. "I'm pitching Bowie tomorrow," he cracked. "Is he right- or left-handed, or does he know?"

If Kuhn were not available, Billy asked, whom would he pitch? "I might go with Alexander—if he gets a haircut," Billy said with a smile. "George asked if the new guys got haircuts. I told him they just got here—give them a chance."

On Friday Kuhn announced his decision. The sale of the three Oakland players would be prohibited "in the best interests of baseball." To permit it "would be devastating to baseball's reputation for integrity and public confidence." Kuhn's decision meant that club owners would be permitted to buy and sell ballplayers as long as they refrained from doing it so blatantly in million-dollar lots. Most owners had urged Kuhn to overrule the sale, fearing the million-dollar price tags would drive up the cost of talent. Once top players found out their worth on the open market, their demands would escalate.

Friday afternoon, after the announcement, gloomy Yankee players milled around the lobby of the Executive House Hotel in Chicago, watching the rain outside and discussing the bad news. A group of reporters stood waiting for the hotel elevator to take them to Martin's twenty-ninth-floor suite where they would ask his reaction to the decision. "This should be a barrel of laughs," one reporter said sourly. "Let's just choose one guy to send in there," another suggested. "The rest of us can wait in the bar."

Martin is always hard to interview. He views reporters with suspicion. They travel with the team, hang around the clubhouse, but they do not always act loyally toward the team. They can stir up trouble. Besides, Martin holds their baseball knowledge in contempt. "If writers knew a goddamn thing, they would be managers," he has said.

After a win, Billy could be congenial, often charming and witty, with the press—until he felt challenged. After one Yankee victory which increased an already healthy lead, a reporter asked Martin if he thought the Yankees might become complacent. "I've never been complacent in my life," Martin said, taking it personally.

"But, I meant . . ." the reporter stumbled, "about your players, Billy."

"How can they get complacent if I'm not?" Martin answered, his eyes narrowing. "I'm their leader, aren't I?" Martin flung the challenge back at the reporter, who was flustered by the menace in Martin's voice. With Martin the physical move seems to lurk closely behind the angry words.

Reporters hated especially to interview Martin when he was unhappy, as he always was after a loss. "The first time you get real gay about losing, you're going to lose all a hundred sixty-two games you play," Martin once explained. "That's why that clubhouse is quiet—a thing called pride."

It is more than pride with Billy. Losing makes him angry. He cannot tolerate it. "A defeat is *never* tolerable," he has said. "If it is, then why the hell do they keep score? They could put zero to zero up on the scoreboard and say, 'Nice game; everybody go home.'"

After a loss Billy's simmering anger seeks an outlet. And he expects sportswriters to respect his bad humor, at least by not asking stupid or tough questions. As he sits in his office sipping a beer, the pauses are long while reporters try to word their questions carefully enough to keep Billy's wrath from falling on them.

The afternoon of Kuhn's ruling, reporters crowded nervously into Martin's hotel suite. Billy sat on a sofa, his feet propped on a coffee table. He spoke calmly but with bitterness. "I can believe Watergate," he said, perhaps forgetting his employer had been fined in a Watergate prosecution. "I can believe those guys' fooling around in Washington, but I can't believe we in baseball who are so intelligent could do something like this.

"We're going to take legal action, strong legal action. The Yankees are going to go after him. George Steinbrenner has tremendous attorneys and he'll go after him," Martin said, perhaps forgetting Steinbrenner's felony conviction despite brilliant work by his lawyers.

"What I got to do first is call a team meeting tonight," Billy continued. He ran a hand through his hair. "My players were up over the fact we got Blue, and I don't want them to be down over not having him.

"What does it mean, 'in the best interest of baseball'?" he continued. "It doesn't mean anything to me. What the commissioner did—the bad publicity we're going to get all over the country—is *that* in the best interests of baseball? Is it in the best interests of baseball to have lawsuits all over the country? The commissioner has opened up a big can of worms, bigger than he imagined."

Billy warmed to his subject while the reporters took notes rapidly. Martin wasn't directing any of his anger at them. His venom was for the commissioner today. Other managers were more accommodating to the press, but other managers did not provide such good copy by attacking the commissioner of baseball. Billy was always willing to take on anyone he felt was against him.

"Apparently somebody's controlling the commissioner pretty good. What's everybody saying?" Someone suggested Walter O'Malley, the Dodger owner who was known to have been against the deal, as one who had Kuhn's ear. "So the American League is run by the National League. I didn't think that would happen," he reflected.

"What upsets me more than anything else is what it's going to do to baseball. I'm in love with baseball. If this person says this isn't in the best interests of baseball, he doesn't know the game I love. Of all the things that have happened, this is the worst thing that has happened in baseball."

None of the reporters challenged Billy Martin's hyperbole. The Yankee front office had only said "no comment" about the decision. Kuhn might well suspend Martin for speaking out, Billy admitted, but he wasn't going to keep quiet.

"Kuhn makes the whole thing sound like a dirty, underhanded deal," he said. "What are general managers supposed to do from now on—call him before they make deals and ask him if it's okay? Will he be calling me to tell me who I can play?"

After the session a few reporters in the hotel bar talked about Martin's overreaction. One mentioned his "persecution complex." Martin has often been accused of treating everyone around him as a potential adversary, but Billy has often been surrounded by people out to get him. If he hadn't scrapped and battled and been ready to take on all comers, he would never have had a chance at success.

When he was a small boy with a large nose, the bigger kids in a tough neighborhood picked on him. As a high-school baseball star, he was overlooked by the major-league scouts. When he was a Yankee, his general manager openly disliked him. When he was a second baseman, opponents slid extra hard into him. When he became a manager, club owners broke their word to him. And Billy fought back all his life. No one and nothing was too big or powerful to intimidate him into silence. Not even the federal government.

Back in the 1950s, when being called to serve in the armed forces was something no right-thinking American would openly question, Billy questioned it—openly and loudly. He believed that his draft board was picking on him, and he had his say.

After his sensational performance in the 1953 World Series, fans in the Bay Area, in Califronia, treated Billy Martin like a hero. In November an Oakland booster club gave Billy a new baby-blue Cadillac. It was Billy's third car. He had acquired his second, a Packard, the month before as a reward for being named Most Valuable Player in the World Series.

Billy was not a hero to everyone in the area, however. People wrote the Berkeley draft board asking why this healthy and apparently wealthy young man wasn't serving his country. They had read about his "hardship" discharge from the Army after very brief service in 1950. It seemed absurd that someone earning about $15,000 as a baseball player, plus more than $8000 for his World Series share, could still be considered a hardship case. In March, 1954, a little more than two months before Martin's twenty-sixth birthday, the age at which he could no longer be drafted, the board reclassified him 1-A.

The day after Billy was reclassified, he spoke by phone with sports columnist Jimmy Cannon in New York. Martin's emotional state was much more stable now than it had been during the '53 season, and he tried, at first, to remain calm about the reclassification and not to complain. "How can I squawk?" he said. "Who the hell can be happy about it? But I can't beef. I got Jerry Coleman's job when he went back into the Marines, didn't I?"

Martin preferred to chat with Cannon about the six weeks he had just spent with Mickey Mantle. "I went up to a hundred eighty-two pounds," he said. "And if I lose it, I'm going to work it off, not worry it off." He told about playing on the local basketball team Mickey coached, complaining lightheartedly because Mantle wouldn't let him play a full game. "What a lousy coach he is," Billy said. "I still got the high-school record in Berkeley for scoring, but you ought to see the way Mickey handled me. I'd make a bucket and

Mickey would yank me. I'd say, 'What the hell's going on?' He'd say, 'Quiet, quiet, I got to concentrate on the game.' Did you ever hear of a lousier coach?"

Cannon asked him again about the draft. "I'd rather play ball, but I'm still young and it's not going to ruin me," Billy said, restraining himself. "I tell you what does trouble me, though. It's the people I'm taking care of."

The more Martin thought about it over the next few days, the more unfair his treatment seemed to be. He had been drafted before, and he had been discharged because he provided the sole support of his mother, his asthmatic stepfather, his younger brother and sister. He still took care of his mother, stepfather, and sister, and now he had an ex-wife and baby daughter depending on him financially. He decided to appeal the draft board's decision.

"I'll fight willingly if they can figure some way to support my dependents," he announced. He drove to the board hearing in his baby-blue Cadillac. Billy had already given the new Packard to Father Dennis Moore, the priest who had helped him and his family when he was a boy. If Martin was hard up for money to support his dependents, the draft board said, he should have sold the car and given his family the money. Plenty of young men served in the Army who were too poor to drive Cadillacs. The board kept Martin classified 1-A and put him at the top of the draft list. They would not even give him credit for the time he had already served in the Army.

"I feel sorry for that draft board," Martin claimed. "They didn't have the courage to stand by my dependency claim."

Billy's battle with the draft board elicited little public support across the nation or in his home area. One San Francisco newspaper received more than three hundred letters attacking Martin's selfishness and lack of patriotism. Even Billy's hometown Berkeley newspaper criticized him.

Martin was inducted into the Army as 1954 spring training began. He spent most of his eighteen months' service at

Fort Carson, near Colorado Springs. Billy was a model soldier. He eventually made corporal and even won a good-conduct medal, which surprised many fans around American League cities. He had his first shot at managing while in the Army, as player-manager of the post team. He also coached two Little League teams in the area.

At the time Billy was in the service, Congressman William E. Hess, of Ohio, conducted investigations of the "coddling" of athletes by the Army. Martin, who felt that he had been given a hard time, wrote a letter to Hess spelling out his complaints. If he was coddled, so was General Jonathan Wainwright after Corregidor, he wrote, referring to the infamous Death March during World War II. Hess looked into Martin's situation and came to no conclusions. Private Martin's gripes didn't receive sympathetic treatment in the press. Mickey Mantle went out to Colorado to visit Billy, and, according to some reports, he urged his buddy to quiet down with his complaints.

Martin was discharged from the Army at the end of August, 1955, in time to lead the second-place Yankees to another pennant. He was still bitter. "You know, I'm broke after two years in the Army," he said. "I'm sore at the draft board. If they threw me out of the Army the first time for having five dependents, why did they put me back in again with five dependents? . . . Because I got my name in the papers and they didn't have guts enough to stand having people ask why I wasn't in the service. I'm glad to serve my country—but why didn't they just leave me in the first time?

"It's tough on a baseball player," he continued. "Right now I'm twenty-seven years old and I've got nothing in the world but my name and my daughter."

He had sold his baby-blue Cadillac.

Chapter 8
HAPPY DAYS

The Yankees missed New York's Bicentennial celebration. On July 4, 1976, barks, brigs, and schooners from around the world sailed up the Hudson River in a stately procession. Across the nation people watched "Operation Sail" on television and saw New Yorkers clustered together on docks and rooftops, cheering, drinking, and enjoying a rare moment of unity. To New Yorkers that day, the ships from the past were a sign that the nation and the city had finally reached a turning point. The absent Yankees were part of the reason New Yorkers felt good about themselves and their city for a change. The Yankees were in first place, just like in the good old days, leading the Eastern Division by eight games over the Cleveland Indians. New York City was happy.

Five hundred miles away, the Yankees took batting practice in Cleveland's Municipal Stadium. The most distinctive sound in all of sports—that of a bat hitting a baseball—cracked through the slowly filling ballpark. In the distance dozens of firecrackers echoed each practice hit.

96

Players awaiting their turns in the batting cage exchanged lighthearted insults. The Yankees were happy.

Near second base a lean man wearing an old infielder's glove yelled "Mine!" and scooped up a grounder. A player standing nearby made a comment about aging reflexes, and the manager laughed. Billy Martin was happy.

The Yankees and their manager could afford to be happy. They were winning. Winning means doing what you are supposed to do. Winning means a shot at the big money of the playoffs and the World Series. Winning is all Billy Martin ever demanded out of life or a ballclub.

There were some strains among the players and their manager, as there are in any collection of individuals making up a team. The shared pleasures of winning made the strains seem unimportant. "We have fun together," said Thurman Munson. "We like each other. In the past there were factions, cliques, a division on the team. Some guys didn't like each other. There were times when guys choked in games or thought more about themselves than the team. But this ballclub is fun. This ballclub is together."

Martin has spoken with pride about lessening the distance between players and manager. He displeased Minnesota owner Calvin Griffith by drinking and playing cards with his players. He violated the old custom of not allowing the players to drink in the hotel bar where the manager drank. "That was the old rule," Martin said, "but it wasn't my rule. I never sat down with my players, buddy-buddy. But I sit at the end of the bar and send them over a round of drinks. Why should I treat them like men on the field and then like boys off the field?"

For a team to be together, an exchange of thoughts is necessary. Many players, though not all of them, felt that Martin communicated well with them. "You can go in and talk with him man to man," said Roy White, the senior Yankee. "I've talked with him a few times when I had things on my mind and I've found good rapport." Communication is easi-

est when there are few serious problems that need to be
talked about, and on the first-place Yankees the problems
were few.

The Yankee players, like Billy's previous players, appreciated Martin for his loyalty. "He sticks up for you," said
Chris Chambliss. "He asks you to do something, he stands
by you." Unlike some managers, Martin would not pass the
buck to his players when questioned by reporters. He might
bawl a player out in private, but he would defend him to the
press and the front office.

With his team winning, Martin could occasionally have
fun with his players, sometimes even acting as flaky as
they did. When rookie sensation Mark "The Bird" Fidrych,
of Detroit, was scheduled to pitch against the Yankees,
Martin ordered a clubhouse attendant to buy some birdseed
to sprinkle around the mound, hoping to attract a flock of
pigeons to distract the pitcher.

On the whole, the team felt close enough to their manager to kid with him. Once, when Martin was late boarding
the team bus, he was greeted with catcalls and insults for
holding the team up. "Give it a rest, you guys," he shouted.
"And knock off the harmonica playing." Yogi Berra, the
manager during the Great Harmonica Incident of 1964,
laughed along with the players.

Dock Ellis liked to jive with Billy, and Billy would jive
him back. "Dock, pitchers are like coconuts on a tree," Martin once explained to Ellis. "If I want another one, all I have
to do is shake the tree."

Graig Nettles has had an easy relationship with his manager. Once, when the Yankees were taking late-afternoon
batting practice in Oakland, Nettles complained that it was
getting hard to see the ball. "Hey, Billy," he said, "can't you
get them to turn the lights on?"

"Yeah," Martin replied, then shouted out to nobody,
"turn on the lights!" Suddenly, the lights came on.

"I always knew you thought you were God," Nettles said. "Now you think you have to prove it."

Comparing the Martin he played for in Denver in 1968 with the Martin of 1976, Nettles said, "Billy's a *little* mellower now. He's learned to take things a *little* easier." Graig thought well of Billy's relations with his players. "He'll still buy players drinks. I like it, running into my manager in restaurants. He doesn't want to be put on a pedestal," Graig said, echoing Martin's favorite expression. Then Nettles added, "In his heart he thinks of himself as one of the players."

In Billy Martin's mind, though, he knew he could not be one of the boys. Martin did not forget the difference between the players and the manager. Billy was the team's boss. And despite the banter, the infield practice, the togetherness, Martin stood apart as the boss. "It's lonely," he has admitted.

As the Fourth of July game with Cleveland began, the Yankee leadoff batter went to the plate. The number-two batter knelt in the on-deck circle. The pitchers and reserve catcher went to the bullpen. The rest of the players sat down on the bench. Billy Martin took his regular position apart from his players. His foot propped on the dugout step, he stared intently at the Cleveland pitcher. Bicentennial Day, a time for memories. . . . Two decades ago, when he and Mickey Mantle and Whitey Ford were the Three Musketeers of the New York Yankees, baseball wasn't lonely for Billy.

Billy Martin's reputation as a devil-may-care, harddrinking swordsman in his Yankee playing days may have been exaggerated. Anyone who didn't drink milk and go to bed at sunset offended the bowl-of-Wheaties image of Yankee purity which George Weiss wanted to project. But

Weiss was correct in believing that Billy spent many late nights having fun with his buddies Mickey and Whitey.

The pressure that drove Billy to prove himself on the field did not let up after the game. He found it almost impossible to relax, and often he couldn't sleep. Drinking, partying, bar-hopping, picking up women—those were his escapes from tension. He found a pair of friends on the Yankees who enjoyed the same kind of fun.

Martin and Whitey Ford, a cocky but easygoing New York City kid, hung around together when they were both twenty-one-year-old rookies in 1950. The next year, Whitey went into the Army and Mickey, a 19-year-old small-town boy, came up to the Yankees. The tough street kid from Berkeley and the hick from Oklahoma became roommates on the road. They also shared an apartment in New York City. When Whitey returned from the Army, in 1953, they became a trio. "We just hit it off right away," Billy said. "I guess we each saw something in the other two and felt we would like to be like them."

In the clubhouse the three would fool around with water pistols and cap guns. Living up to his nickname of Billy the Kid, Martin kept a pair of holsters with toy six-shooters in his locker, and he and Mickey would have quick-draw contests. When Whitey was pitching, Martin would visit the mound frequently. If Whitey was having a hard time, Billy would shake his head and say, "Want me to pitch?"

The three stuck together on the team. Once, in his rookie year, Mantle dropped a fly ball, costing an established Yankee pitching star a victory. "Kid, you'll never make it," the pitcher said to Mickey. "Boy, did I chew that pitcher out," Billy remembered a few years ago, on the day both Mantle and Ford were elected to the Hall of Fame. "I told him he had a lot of guts to talk, the way they were hitting him. I wonder what that guy thinks about Mickey now."

When the game ended, the three would go out on the town. Mantle has said of his roommate, "Billy seemed to be the guy who invented parties. I hadn't finished growing up, and Billy, who was three years older, had probably decided he was not going to. Anyway, we undertook to enjoy life together. And Billy could be just as intense about celebrating as playing."

Some teammates, as well as the front office, worried that the city kids, Martin and Ford, were a bad influence on the potential superstar from the sticks. Pitcher Allie Reynolds spoke about this with Peter Golenbock, author of *Dynasty: The New York Yankees, 1949–1964*. "For a ballplayer in New York City," he said, "there just isn't anything you can't get if you want it. And we had some other kids there. Whitey Ford and Billy Martin. They weren't too helpful to him. Really. Also, because Mickey was a country boy, people would take advantage of him."

On the other hand, Virgil Trucks, who roomed with Martin in Kansas City, thought Martin was the patsy for the other two, since Billy always took the blame for whatever trouble they all got into. Martin's role as scapegoat, however, probably was not the fault of his friends. Stars always get away with more than nonstars do, in any field. And Billy was the only one of the Three Musketeers who wasn't an All-Star. In fact, fans would often treat Billy as Mickey's representative. "I can't remember the number of times I've been confused with the mascot," he said at the time. "Often, coming out of the park, kids and girls have asked me to get Mickey's autograph for them. And I always accept. Mickey gets a big kick out of it. It's getting to be an act."

"Mickey and I used to tease Billy that he was leading us astray," Whitey said. "But that wasn't the case. I don't believe that any one of us led the others astray. The three of us just got along real good together."

According to Whitey, Billy wasn't even a very big drinker. "I nurse a drink so long," Billy once claimed, "that bartenders say to me, 'Want to put that in a container to take home?'" To keep up with his buddies in ordering rounds,

Billy would often dump his drinks when Whitey and Mickey weren't looking. Once, Billy poured his drink into a nearby fire bucket while the other two were at the bar ordering another round. When they returned, Mickey asked him, "Where's your drink?"

"I finished it," Billy said, pointing to his empty glass.

"If you did," Mantle said, "how come you don't even have ice cubes left in your glass?"

The three would drink to their capacities, and then some. Once, in Chicago, they went to a Polynesian restaurant and had three giant rum drinks. By the time they finished the third, they realized their train was about to leave, so they ran the five blocks to the station. Then, in the minutes before the train left, Mickey and Billy began wrestling, one of their favorite pastimes. By the time the train pulled out, both were throwing up in the aisles.

All too often the trio's late-night activities came to the attention of the front office. When the Yankees clinched the 1953 pennant, with Billy Martin driving in four runs, the usual champagne celebration was held in the clubhouse. Then Martin, Mantle, and Ford, plus a few other Yankees, decided to continue celebrating elsewhere. They chose the Latin Quarter, a flashy New York nightclub.

When the waiter brought the bill at the end of the evening, Billy offered to pay the whole thing himself, even though it came to almost $100. The others insisted on chipping in. Not everybody, however, had enough to cover his share. Whitey had a better idea. He grabbed the bill and signed Dan Topping's name to it, since the Yankee co-owner was sitting at another table nearby. Whitey also signed his, Mantle's, and Martin's names, leaving off the other Yankees, to keep them out of trouble. The high-spirited trio figured it was a prank they could get away with, having just clinched the Yankees' fifth straight pennant.

Dan Topping did not think it was funny. He slapped $500 fines on each of the three. After the Series victory over the

Dodgers, the Yankees held a celebration party, and Billy and Mickey cornered Topping at the bar. Billy, at his most charming, suggested that the $500 fine was a little steep for such an innocent mistake. Topping pulled out a checkbook and wrote each of them a check for $500. Billy then found Whitey and told him, "Go over and ask Topping for the five hundred dollars—he'll write you a check." "Tell him to stick it up his ass," Whitey said. Ford was often the coolest customer of the three.

Once, though, Billy led Whitey into a situation that almost blew Whitey's city-slicker cool. A group of Yankees were drinking at a nightclub in East St. Louis when Billy got into an argument, as often happened. This time it was with the bartender, and Ralph Houk, then a reserve catcher noted for his toughness, quickly joined in. Ford, who had been away from the others, watching the stage show, saw that a brawl was about to break out and hurried over. Just then the owner of the nightclub came over and pulled a gun out of his pocket. Houk roared, "That don't scare me," and picked up a bottle. The owner, still clutching his gun, retreated to his office in the back. "That may not have scared Ralph but it sure scared me," Ford said.

Casey Stengel rarely bothered with curfews. Once, in Boston, however, after a number of losing games, he announced an eleven-thirty curfew that would be strictly enforced. The first night of the curfew Billy and Mickey came back late to the Kenmore Hotel, where the team stayed in Boston. They spotted Casey in the lobby, passing the time of night with newspapermen. There was no way to sneak by the manager, so they turned around and headed down an alley, which they knew led to a back door. The door was locked. Billy suggested he climb up on Mickey's back so he could squeeze through a window above the door. Then he would open the door to let Mickey in.

Billy made it through the window and Mickey waited. And waited. Finally Billy popped his head out the window, said, "I can't open it; good night, Mickey," and disappeared. Before Billy could unlock the door to their room, he heard a loud crash as Mickey failed in his first attempt to reach the window by piling up garbage cans. A few minutes later, though, Mickey made it through the window, and walked into the room, smelling like a garbage truck, furious at his giggling roommate.

Weiss once thought about separating the roommates, but he never did. His reasoning probably went along the same lines as Billy's. "Why bother?" Martin said. "We'll just keep two other guys out late."

Casey Stengel wasn't one to lay all the blame for poor playing on lack of clean living. At one team meeting called to bawl out his players, he didn't mention any names but covered everybody in his category of offenses: "Now first, you lovers," he said. "You single guys who are out chasing something all night and you married guys who are telling girls you're single . . . " Casey went on and explained how sex doesn't hurt a player, but staying up all night looking for it does. "And you drinkers . . . " he continued, hitting some of his players more than once. "I'm the only one who's going to stay up all night drinking." Casey wasn't through yet. "And you churchgoers and milk-shake drinkers. Now, it's fine to have some of you guys on a team, but if you don't start showing me some guts out there, if you don't play hard enough for me, I'm going to make every one of you go out and get a double Scotch and a woman!"

One reason Casey rarely complained to Billy, Mickey, and Whitey about their nightlife was that he knew they were such intense competitors they could probably use some loosening up after a game. Casey had to get on them occasionally about being too intense. One time, after Mickey had been particularly vicious in kicking the water cooler following a strikeout, Casey made a speech about how baseball should be fun. You had to get fun out of it to stay loose and do your best, he said.

Billy and Mickey decided to take Stengel up on this idea. Martin was the next to strike out, so when he came back into the dugout, he said, "A mile over my head!" and laughed. Mickey joined in the merriment over Billy's strikeout. They kept it up for a few more strikeouts while Casey watched them sourly. Finally he snarled, "That's enough of that."

Some of the wildest partying the Yankees ever did together came after the 1955 season when they made a tour of Japan, playing Japanese baseball teams. In one town the team held a party in their hotel bar and invited servicemen from the local American Air Force base. At four in the morning everyone had gone to bed except Billy, Whitey, and Don Larsen. Martin came up with a scheme to revive the party. He picked up the phone, and while Ford and Larsen banged chairs together, Martin called each player's room and said, "There's a big fight in the bar with the Air Force guys! We need help—hurry down!"

The Yankees rushed out of their rooms and down to the bar, dressed in underwear, kimonos and pajamas. Billy's plan worked. Most of them stayed on drinking and laughing and finally having breakfast together. Don Larsen, who was an even more notorious partier than Martin, had the last laugh. He signed Billy's name to all the bar bills.

Mickey, Whitey, and Billy did not limit their companionship to the baseball season. They would visit one another during the off-season, too. Mickey and Billy even had a dream of buying a ranch together someday, to be called the M&M. Once, the three of them went on a hunting trip in Texas. They were driving over a rocky road in a 1930 Model-T Ford, heading for a deer hunting area, when suddenly a deer bounded out into the road. Billy, who was driving, stopped the car and jumped out to the left, rifle at the ready, and Mickey jumped out to the right. Whitey stayed in the car, aimed his rifle and fired between his teammates. Billy and Mickey dived in opposite directions with loud curses for their friend. They didn't trust the New York City kid's aim with a rifle as well as his aim with a fastball.

"Every time I think of that, I shudder," Whitey remembered with a grin. "I almost wiped out the Yankee team."

Billy Martin, Mickey Mantle, and Whitey Ford shared success and fame early in their twenties. They partied late into the night as if driven by a fear it could not last. For Mantle and Ford, it lasted a long time. For Billy, it did not.

Chapter 9
THE END OF A YANKEE

On August 4, 1976, the Yankees returned home after a disappointing road trip. It was a Monday, and Billy Martin was feeling blue. Though his team had a 9½ game lead, the Yankees had lost six of their last seven games. The sports pages were speculating on the possibility of a Yankee collapse, and Billy was growing more edgy with each loss. It didn't help his mood when before the night game with Detroit he looked up at the owner's box and saw Dick Williams sitting there with George Steinbrenner.

Dick Williams had been Steinbrenner's first choice as Yankee manager, shortly after George and his Cleveland group bought the club from CBS. When Ralph Houk resigned, at the end of the 1973 season, Steinbrenner offered Williams a multiyear contract. But Charles O. Finley, under whom Williams had managed the Oakland A's to two straight world championships, changed his mind about letting Williams out of his contract and quashed the deal. Steinbrenner had to settle on a second choice—Bill Virdon, of the Pirates—for the 1974 season. When Virdon was fired, in 1975, Williams was managing the California Angels. Recently, he had been fired from that job, and now presumably he was job hunting. And there he was, chatting with his old admirer George Steinbrenner.

Billy Martin was on his way to winning the Eastern Division championship in his first full season as Yankee skipper, so he had nothing to worry about. And yet—Billy Martin had been fired as a winner before. . . . Williams was appearing at the low point in Yankee fortunes. . . . Steinbrenner had a reputation for firing employees who didn't meet his very high standards of performance . . . . And Martin still hadn't been offered a new contract. Billy was "mad," he admitted later.

Many observers had been waiting for conflict to develop between Steinbrenner and Martin. It just couldn't last, this surface calm between the two. Martin had made a habit of sounding off at front-office executives, and George M. Steinbrenner was just the type for Martin to clash with— impatient, strong, abrasive, a dominant owner. They were too much alike to last in a boss-employee relationship.

The prime conflict between Martin and his former bosses had always centered on what he termed "clubhouse interference." Billy demands that he as manager have absolute authority over his players, on the field and off. If a general manager or owner wants to deal with a player, he should go through the manager. Otherwise, he is "back-dooring," says Billy.

As principal owner, Steinbrenner sees himself not as a figure in the background but as the leader. "If you're going to lead, then, goddamn it, *lead*," he has said.

Once, during the season, Steinbrenner called a meeting of the Yankee pitching staff to bawl them out for poor performance. That was just the type of "interference" that can light Martin's short fuse, but this time Billy restrained himself.

"The team was going bad and I thought it was time to say

something," George later explained. "As long as you're paying the bills, you've got a right to be heard. I asked Billy if it was okay, and I talked to them in his office. He was right there. And believe me, I was tough. I was bad. I wanted them so teed off, they'd say, 'I'll show that SOB.'"

Sometime later a reporter informed Martin that since the Steinbrenner pep talk, the starting pitchers had a collective earned run average of 2.31. Billy said, "I'm very happy." However, the scrunched-up expression on his face revealed another reaction.

The two nights that Williams sat in Steinbrenner's box he watched the Yankees defeat the Tigers twice. Then the Yankees resumed their slumping ways, losing five of their next six games. Finally they snapped out of it with a five-game winning streak. Still there was no announcement about Martin's contract.

Rumors persisted that Dick Williams was about to join the Yankees in some capacity. The Yankee front office was run smoothly by Gabe Paul, who didn't seem to need help. Everyone knew that if Williams were hired, it would be as manager or as manager-in-waiting—in case Billy faltered down the stretch.

Steinbrenner denied any thought of replacing his manager. And yet, he held off offering a new contract. "It's no big thing. I'm not upset. I'm more concerned about winning games," Martin said. "More wins and it would be hard for them not to give me a contract. Look at our attendance at home and on the road."

Back in the clubhouse, the players were beginning to wonder. "How can they not give him a new contract when they see the way the team's going, and the job he's done?" asked one. Another player added, "There's no doubt he'd like to know about a new contract, and so would we. It might take some pressure off him, relax all of us, be a boost in the pennant race for him and us if they would let him know."

Whatever Billy was thinking, for once he was not saying it publicly. If anything did go wrong between George and him, it would not be the first time a Yankee executive named George had truncated Billy's Yankee career.

George Weiss, Yankee general manager, had been determined to get rid of Martin ever since 1950, when the brash rookie had the audacity to yell at Weiss for sending him down to the minors. Billy was Casey's boy, and Weiss knew Casey had power with the owners, Del Webb and Dan Topping. He couldn't be rash in trading Billy. He had to have a good reason or an excellent trade to make. The fact that Martin became a valuable player for the Yankees made Weiss's goal more difficult.

At the end of the 1953 season, when Martin was hero of the World Series, Casey felt called upon to defend his boy publicly against the Yankee management. "He's a real good ballplayer," Casey told an Oakland gathering. "And I don't mean just that he can field, throw, run bases, hit, make the double play, and win ballgames. I also mean he's good for the manager, good for the coaches, good for his teammates, and good for the owners. Now, I wish the owners would realize this and quit bothering me about the kid." When Casey said owners, he meant the owner's representative, George Weiss. Topping and Webb themselves rarely interfered in Weiss's operation of the club.

Weiss would use any excuse to assert his power over Billy. At spring training one year, the general manager called Martin to his office. Weiss showed Billy a letter he had received from the mother of a girl Billy had dated over the winter. "I didn't know big-league players were allowed to go into nightclubs," the mother complained. Weiss asked Martin to explain. Billy laughed. "Are you kidding me?" he said. "Look, I'm single. I'm divorced. What's wrong with me taking a girl to a nightclub, especially over the winter?

What I do with my time in the winter is my business."

Weiss concluded the meeting by telling Martin, "All right, you can do what you want in the winter, but I'm warning you—you watch yourself during the season."

Weiss watched Billy. He even hired private detectives to watch Billy and some of his teammates. The detectives eventually became a joke with the players. "One day one of those dicks missed me when I went out of the hotel," Billy remembered, "so I turned back into the lobby, tapped him on the shoulder, and said, 'Hey, fella, I'm leaving. Come on.'"

In the spring of 1957 Weiss laid it even heavier on Martin. He said, "I hate to tell you this, but you have trouble just once and we'll do something drastic."

"I tried to get along with Weiss," Billy complained. "I tried everything but kiss his boots." One thing Weiss did not like about Martin was knowing that Billy would never kiss his boots.

Billy was worried enough as it was going into the 1957 season. The '56 season had not been a good one for him, at bat or in the field. He blamed it on his Army service, which caused him to miss the 1954 season and most of 1955. "I found it a tough road," he said about his return. "I was okay physically and I could handle the general mechanics of baseball. What was hard was the thinking. Plays that came easy before I now was handling the wrong way. It wasn't until about August of last season that I got into the groove. I'm straightened out again and believe that this season should be my best—in hitting, in fielding, and in thinking. I'm twenty-eight and ready for my peak."

He had to be good in '57, for a major threat to Billy's job appeared in spring camp that year. The brightest product of the Yankee farm system, Bobby Richardson, was a slick-fielding, good-hitting, clean-living second baseman. Feeling on the defensive, Billy acted brasher than ever. When New York *Post* sports columnist Milt Gross asked Martin to rate the league's second baseman, Billy demanded, "Who's better than me?" Nellie Fox, then the annual All-Star selection, was suggested. "What's he got over me except average? You don't believe me, you ask the other guys." Billy called over Jerry Coleman and Phil Rizzuto, the latter just starting his broadcasting career. He asked them to explain the difference between himself and the other second basemen in the league. Both graciously accommodated Billy. While Martin prompted with questions and nodded his head at their answers, Phil and Jerry explained how Billy made the double play better, came up with the big plays, and was always doing something extra out there at second.

Early in the '57 season, Martin was moved to third base to fill in for Andy Carey, who had sprained his ankle. Twenty-one-year-old Bobby Richardson played second, and played it well. Martin kidded Bobby, telling him that he'd written his draft board and that Bobby should be hearing from them soon, or that he'd slipped something in Bobby's milk that morning which should affect him before game time.

Billy's twenty-ninth birthday was coming up on May 16, and some of his friends on the team decided to celebrate the occasion with Billy by going out on the town on May 15, the night before an open day on the schedule. The party that met at Danny's Hideaway for dinner that night included Martin, Mickey Mantle, Whitey Ford, Hank Bauer, Yogi Berra, and young pitcher Johnny Kucks, feeling honored but uncomfortable to be included among the in-group. Billy came without a date and the others all brought their wives. After dinner the group went to a show at the Waldorf Astoria and then on to the Copacabana, one of New York's most expensive nightclubs, to hear Sammy Davis, Jr.

At the Copa, the Yankee party was seated near a group of bowlers out to celebrate the end of their team's season. One of the bowlers, a fat delicatessen owner from the Bronx who'd had more than a few drinks, began to heckle Sammy Davis, Jr. Hank Bauer, the tough ex-Marine, was seated closest to the bowlers and told the fat man to shut up. More remarks were exchanged between the tables.

The Yankee wives urged their husbands to stay out of trouble. But tempers fueled by alcohol were short. Finally, Billy threw out the challenge, suggesting that the dispute be settled elsewhere. The men at both tables stood up quickly and headed for the nearest door, which led into a men's room. One of the bowlers—the deli owner's brother— decided to play peacemaker. He approached Billy and promised to shut up the fat man if the Yankees would keep Bauer away from him. As Martin and the peacemaker were talking, Bauer and the bowlers were already in the adjoining men's room, along with several Copa bouncers who had hurried over when they saw trouble starting. By the time Billy arrived, the deli owner was out cold on the floor. Bauer later swore he never hit the man and it must have been the bouncers who'd worked him over.

The Yankees left the club as fast as they could, escorted through a kitchen exit by Copa personnel. New York *Post* gossip columnist Leonard Lyons spotted them leaving and began asking questions. At four-thirty in the morning a police reporter from the *Daily News* called Hank Bauer to tell him a fat man was at a local precinct swearing out a warrant for Bauer's arrest on assault and battery. This charge eventually led to a grand-jury hearing, at which all the Yankees involved testified. The grand jury did not find enough evidence to return an indictment against Bauer or any of the others. But the grand jury was only one of the players' worries.

After the morning *Daily News* appeared with the headline BAUER IN BRAWL AT COPA, the six Yankees were summoned to Weiss's office. All of them told the same story: "Nobody did nothing to nobody," in Yogi's words. Weiss was not satisfied: maybe the players had a right to go out with their wives, but something unsavory had happened. And Weiss was sure Martin had been responsible.

Mantle told Billy, "You didn't do anything. You won't be blamed." And Ford agreed. "Don't worry," he said. "Everybody knows you weren't even in the room." Billy Martin knew better. He knew he would be blamed. His only hope was that Casey would stand by him.

Casey's comment on the whole Copa incident was phrased in his typically obscure way: "The reason they held the party there was that they didn't want to hold it in a hospital."

Weiss fined Martin, Mantle, Ford, Berra, and Bauer $1,000 each, while Kucks, who made considerably less money than the stars, was fined $500. Since the fines were levied before the grand-jury hearing, they seemed to imply that the six Yankees were guilty. The players resented this. Martin leaked the amount of the fines to the press, which Weiss resented.

The trading deadline, June 15, was four weeks away. Martin hoped he would make it through the deadline, but he knew it wasn't likely. Weiss now had his excuse to rid himself of Martin. And Billy was not even in the starting lineup anymore. Carey had returned to third, and Richardson was playing so well at second that Stengel kept Martin on the bench for most games.

Martin joked with reporters about being traded; then he explained, "You know I'm kidding. I'd hate to leave this club. But I expect it, and it's all part of the game." Martin was bracing his neck, and his heart, for the falling ax, waiting and waiting as the June 15 deadline drew closer and closer.

On the eve of the deadline the Yankees arrived in Kansas City, home of the Athletics since 1955, a favorite breeding ground for prospective Yankees and dumping ground for dispensable Yankees. Trade rumors buzzed more loudly. "I feel like a condemned man about to eat his last meal,"

Billy said as he stepped off the team bus at the ball park. He checked the lineup card, and when he saw he wasn't on it, he went out to the bullpen to wait. In the sixth inning, Casey called for him and Billy came.

"Well, you're gone," Casey told him. "You were the smartest little player I ever had." Billy said nothing. "After the game I'm going to call in Arnold Johnson and Parke Carroll," Casey continued, speaking of the Kansas City owners, "and tell them how great a ballplayer you are and how I think the world of you."

"You'll do nothing," Martin said, rejecting Casey's last gesture. He turned and walked into the locker room.

The trade sent Martin and three young prospects—Woodie Held, Bob Martyn and Ralph Terry—to the Athletics for a thirty-three-year-old lefty hitting outfielder, Harry "Suitcase" Simpson, plus fireballing pitcher Ryne Duren. As anxious as Weiss had been to dump Martin, he had not made a bad trade. Simpson did not turn out to be of much value to the team, but Ryne Duren eventually did. With his super fastball, his wildness, his thick glasses and his reputation for drinking, he frightened batters enough to become a very effective relief pitcher. Bobby Richardson would have been the Yankees' second baseman even if Martin had not been traded.

There was another purpose in the trade—to scare the other members of Martin's gang. Weiss knew Martin could not be a bad influence without some cooperation on the part of Ford and Mantle, and he couldn't afford to part with them. He hoped they would now see the error of their high-living ways.

After the game with Kansas City, Mickey Mantle cried in the locker room. "It's like losing a brother," he said. "Billy was the best friend I had." Whitey also had tears in his eyes. All the Yankees thought it was a bad deal. Enos Slaughter was incredulous. "For Simpson? Somebody's crazy." Casey Stengel admitted he thought Kansas City had got the best of the trade. Later, when the front-office announcement stated that Simpson would be the new Yankee left fielder, Casey said, "I'll play who *I* want."

On the bus trip back to the hotel the Yankee players were silent. Martin, riding the bus for the last time, saw Bobby Richardson sitting alone. Billy went over and sat down next to him. "You're going great, kid," Billy said. "You've got it made." Billy, Mickey, and Whitey stayed up the whole night together, talking and drinking and remembering.

Billy Martin was always at his best on the field when his emotional state was in turmoil and when he had something to prove. The next day, he reported to the Kansas City clubhouse. He put on an Athletics uniform. And he started the game at second base for Kansas City, playing against his old teammates. In the fourth inning he hit a single. In the eighth, with the score tied, he hit a home run. The Yankees, however, went on to win in extra innings.

"It was sure strange playing against those guys," he said after the game. "When I hit the home run, I didn't know whether to be happy or cry," he said, his voice breaking a little. "It's strange being in another uniform. I never wore any other in the majors. And, you know, I was with Stengel for two years before that."

For the next six years Martin refused to speak to Casey. "My heart was broke, because I felt that a father, not just a manager, had let me down," he said.

Over those years, Casey would shout to Billy across baseball diamonds, walk beside him in ballpark runways, greet him in hotel lobbies. But Billy wouldn't speak. In 1961, after Casey had been fired by the Yankees, Martin wrote an article for *Sport* magazine entitled "I Loved That Old Man." The article expressed Billy's deep feelings of affection and gratitude toward Casey. It showed regret, not anger. Still, for another two years Billy did not speak to his mentor. Then, during the 1963 winter baseball meetings in Houston, Billy walked up to Casey in a hotel lobby and said, "Hi,

Casey." Stengel was shocked, but just for a moment. He jumped up and began talking and talking, as he always did, as if not a day had passed that they hadn't spoken.

Billy never forgot his bitterness toward Weiss. "The only thing that hurts me is that tag 'bad influence,'" he once told a reporter.

"Well," he was asked, "do you think you influenced Mantle?"

"Sure," Martin replied. "We roomed together and hung around together and he led the league in everything. I only wish he influenced me like I influenced him. How can you be a bad influence on six pennant winners? It don't strike me as fair that a guy should be rapped as a bad influence by people who don't even know what they're talking about. It's a serious thing and there's nothing I can do about it. You get the rap, you're stuck. It isn't fair."

Martin's old World Series rival Jackie Robinson came to his defense. "Billy is not a Dead End Kid," Jackie said, "or any of the other things he has been called. He is a smart player, always thinking, always daring, always looking for a way to win. A player like that gets to be a pain in the neck to some people, I presume, but it has nothing to do with the man. He has always played up to the fullest the times I played against him."

Kansas City acquired Billy hoping he would spark the team out of its faltering ways. The next time they visited Yankee Stadium, the Athletics were on a losing streak. "Some spark plug," Martin said. "I'm a spark plug in reverse. I spark them to eleven losses."

Whitey Ford was pitching that day, and late in the game the Yankees had a big lead. When Billy came up, Whitey threw him a big, slow curve, which Martin took for a strike. As Ford went into his windup again, he called to his old buddy, "Same pitch." Martin hit it for a home run. That didn't happen every time Martin faced Ford, however. Once, Whitey knocked him down with a brush-back pitch.

"You keep that up and your kids won't get any Christmas presents," Billy yelled at him. "Who needs them?" Whitey yelled back. "They're cheap toys, anyway."

Martin did his best for the Athletics, even though he batted only .251 with 39 RBIs that year, and he missed many games because of injuries. "I said to myself, I'm going to make up for it," he explained. "I said I'll try harder at Kansas City. I'll bust my tail for them." But it wasn't the same on a losing team. His sparks could not ignite players inured to defeat.

"It gets so you start in telling the other guys what to do," Billy said. "Then you stop yourself and say, what am I trying to do? I ought to mind my business. It's hard to get up, to get excited, when you know the game don't mean too much.

"You get used to winning," he added. "You like it. You can't help feeling it, and you can't help feeling the comedown."

Before one late-season game at Yankee Stadium, Billy went over to a first-row box to greet Francis Cardinal Spellman, then archbishop of New York. "How do you like it in Kansas City, Billy?" the Cardinal asked warmly. "Oh, just fine, Your Eminence," Billy replied, then walked back to the batting cage, muttering under his breath.

The Cardinal could as well have asked Billy how he would have liked to be excommunicated from the Catholic Church.

A quarter century ago, Billy Martin's nose was larger and his smile broader, but the pinstripes were the same.

Photos courtesy of The New York Yankees except where otherwise noted

A fearsome Billy poses for action shot during his first Yankee spring training in 1950.

Above: Charlie Dressen congratulates Casey Stengel on acquiring Billy, who played for both managers in the minors. Right: Corporal Martin, a Little League manager, corrects the position of a player's baseball cap. Below: His unwelcomed Army hitch delayed Billy's receiving the 1953 World Series MVP award until 1955.

Yankees photo by Bob Olen

If the postmark wasn't New York, Billy's mail probably wasn't from a fan.

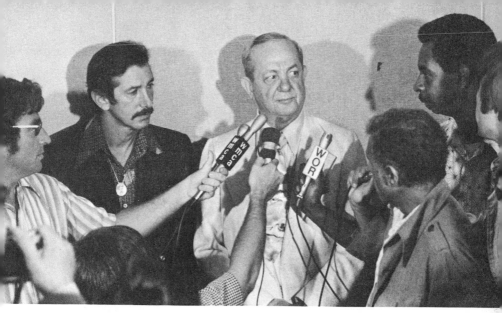

Above: Billy listens intently as Yankee president Gabe Paul explains to reporters why Martin was hired as manager. Below: Martin's new cap as Yankee manager delights his old buddy Mickey Mantle.

In 1975, mustachioed Martin looks more like an old gun fighter ready for a quick draw than a manager.

During Old Timers Day, 1975, Mickey and Billy share a joke too private for Joe DiMaggio's ears.

Always a charmer of ladies, young and old, Billy greets Mrs. Babe Ruth at the reopening of Yankee Stadium.

The umpire seems to have misjudged the call by at least two feet, according to Martin.

In the Yankee dugout, things can often look grim, even to a winning manager.

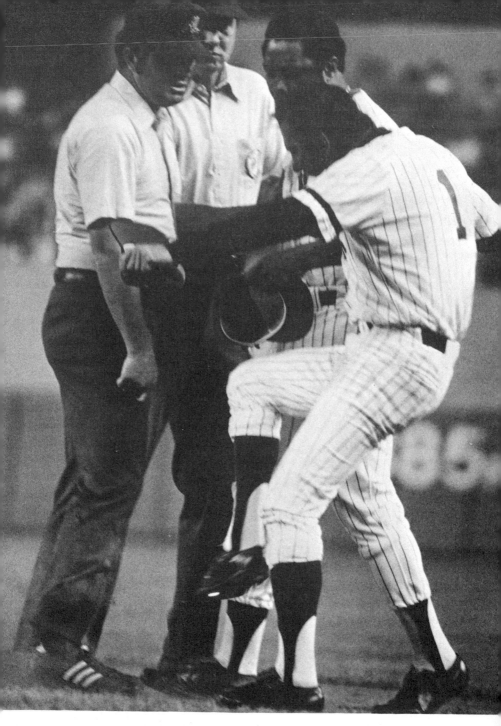

Martin amplifies on his differing view to the umpire.

Yankee number one rushes into the fray, ready to argue for his player.

Chapter 10
BOUNCING AROUND LIKE
A BALL

Loud, angry words could be heard coming from the Yankee dugout on Old-Timers' Day, August 7, 1976. Billy Martin had just lifted pitcher Doyle Alexander after Alexander had given up four runs and seven hits to the Baltimore Orioles in four innings. The intense pitcher was angry with his manager. "They were *horseshit* hits! My arm's as good as it was last time," he shouted, referring to his previous start, a two-hit shutout. "*I* decide how your arm is," Billy yelled back, "not you!"

The manager's neck muscles tightened and his hands balled into fists. The other players, none of whom had ever dared yell at Martin, watched in amazement, waiting for Billy's volcanic temper to erupt and, possibly, for punches to fly. Alexander knew that Martin wasn't a man to challenge, but Doyle's ego and pride had been attacked. His manager had showed no faith in him, just after Doyle thought he had finally proved himself as a pitcher. Alexander didn't want a fight, so he turned away and walked into the tunnel to the clubhouse.

Doyle Alexander believed in himself. He was an egoist, as all pitchers must be. You have to have a strong ego to choose a position from which you control 90 percent of a game.

Doyle had been stuck in the role of relief pitcher during most of his major-league career, which began in 1971, when he was twenty. All the while he knew that if he got a real shot at it, he could be a twenty-game winner. When Baltimore wouldn't pay him what he knew he was worth, he refused to sign a contract for the 1976 season, and the Orioles included him in the June 15 trade with New York.

On his second start with the Yankees, Alexander retired the first 21 batters he faced before being bombed in the eighth. Five starts later he retired the first 14 batters. The next time out he put down 17 straight before being forced out. Then came his two-hit shutout, in which he had a perfect game for 6⅔ innings. And now his manager wouldn't let him work though a shaky start.

Billy Martin learned early in his baseball career that pitchers were the most peculiar and individualistic of all baseball players. To get the best out of one, you have to chew him out; another, you have to coddle. Billy learned this as a Yankee second baseman trotting over to the mound to deal with a pitcher in trouble. He would say to Tom Sturdivant, "Why, you big pussy, Molly Putz could hit you. You could hit me right in my nose with your fastball and it wouldn't hurt." And Sturdivant would become angry enough to throw harder. With Whitey Ford, Billy would ease the tension by kidding. To Vic Raschi, Martin hardly said a word. Raschi was so intense a pitcher Billy knew he should be left alone during a game.

Martin also knew no player could be allowed to yell at his manager in front of the team. After the game, Billy ordered the clubhouse door locked for a team meeting. His voice tense, his eyes fixed mostly on Alexander, the Yankee manager explained who was boss. "A player *never* talks back to the manager, not in front of the other players," Billy said. "I have an office with a door for that." If anyone did it again, Martin promised, "I'll kick the crap out of him right there in front of the team."

"We had our discussion," was all Doyle would say after the meeting. "A pitcher got angry because I took him out," his manager said. "It's resolved now."

The night before Alexander's next scheduled start, he walked into Martin's office and asked to speak with him. Billy told him to shut the door and sit down. Doyle had been thinking about the blowup, he said, and he wanted to apologize to Billy. He still believed he shouldn't have been lifted, but he knew he was wrong to say what he did. Billy smiled. He accepted the apology.

"He was very much a gentleman," Martin said later. "He came in here and he didn't have to. It was all settled and yet he apologized to me."

The next day, August 11, Doyle Alexander took the mound against the Kansas City Royals. The first three batters Doyle faced hit a single, a home run and a triple. Martin reached for the phone and ordered Dick Tidrow to start throwing in the bullpen. The fourth Royal batter popped out. Then Alexander saw that familiar sight—Billy Martin walking out to the mound. Doyle stared at the ground, but Martin was just out there for a visit. He told the pitcher to be careful with the next hitter, Hal McRae. Doyle already knew to be careful of McRae, who was hitting in the mid–three hundreds. Actually Martin made his trip to the mound only to give Tidrow more time to warm up. McRae singled a runner home for the third run of the inning but was tagged out after making a turn at first. "Alexander can thank McRae for getting picked off," Martin said later. "If he had stayed on base, I would have replaced him."

Despite the four hits and three runs, the manager left his pitcher in. Alexander bore down, and he proved he could pitch himself out of trouble. The Yankees scored five runs in the second, and Doyle allowed no more runs and only four more hits before he was lifted in the ninth when he had trouble with the final out. Sparky Lyle took care of that job for him with one pitch, and Doyle had won his game, 5–3.

After the game Martin said, "I understand how he felt Saturday. He wanted to beat Baltimore so badly. You know how it is when a team trades you away. But tonight wasn't even related to last Saturday. You can't carry hard feelings when somebody expressed his opinion and you disagree. If you keep these things going, everybody would hate everybody else in baseball."

One person who knew how it felt to be traded, and who hated Billy Martin for it, had just pitched against the Yankees that night. Ex-Yankee Larry Gura, traded away three months earlier, came in as relief pitcher for Kansas City after the Yankees' five-run outburst in the second. Gura, who allowed only one hit in 7⅓ innings, thought Martin should have had more faith in him when Larry was a Yankee.

"The man screwed me," said Gura. "When I walked off the mound in the ninth, I looked for him in the Yankee dugout to see the expression on his face, but he was already down in the tunnel."

Billy Martin knew how Doyle Alexander felt. He knew how Larry Gura felt. Martin knew the bitterness and frustration of being traded from team to team, never getting settled, never winning the vote of confidence a player needs from his manager.

Billy Martin tried hard for all the six teams he played with in the last five years of his career. But he was, as he phrased it, "bouncing around like a ball. Anybody says he likes to be traded is a liar." And traded he was.

After his '57 season at Kansas City, the Detroit Tigers acquired Billy, paying a high price in three front-line play-

ers. The Tigers had first-rate talent but played like dead
fish and had finished fourth the previous year. They wanted
Martin to provide spark. "Now that we got Martin," said
Jack Tighe, Tiger manager, "we're a pennant contender.
Billy's the kind of guy we needed, a natural leader. He
knows how to win and he'll show the others." Tighe also
had a high opinion of Martin's versatility. He planned to
switch Billy from second to shortstop. Harvey Kuenn, a fine
hitter, was slowing down at short and would be shifted to
center. It all seemed to make sense.

Martin himself expressed pleasure with the trade.
Though he wasn't returning to the Yankees, he was going
from a loser to a winner. "I feel better about being with Detroit," he said. "The Tigers are contenders and a fellow who
has been with the Yankees can't be happy playing on a losing club. But I'm not knocking Kansas City. Playing there
is better than working.

"I feel I can play shortstop," Martin continued. "I don't
have to worry about that long throw in the hole. My arm is
good." He went on to say that the '57 World Series, in which
the Yankees lost to the Milwaukee Braves, showed something. "It shows they're ready to be taken. And Detroit, we
could take them. We got a helluva team."

Others doubted Billy's ability to play short. Gil McDougald, the Yankee shortstop, spoke of the pressures of having to make more plays and therefore more errors than other infielders. "I've got a feeling that Billy is too high-strung
for that position," McDougald said. "The ability to relax after you've made a boot is the toughest part of playing the
position. And you have to acquire it by experience. That's
why it could be tough for Martin to step right in there this
season."

In spring training Martin did his best to live up to his
role as shortstop and spark plug. On one bus trip he led a
songfest for his new teammates and thought it went well.
On the next bus trip he brought along song sheets. At a

spring training game against Milwaukee a reporter asked him if he looked upon this as a preview of the next World Series. "That's about the size of it," Martin said cheerfully. "That is, if the Braves can repeat." In a game against the Yankees, Mickey Mantle hit a grounder to Martin. Billy fielded it, then held the ball, forcing Mickey to race for first, before throwing him out at the last instant. "You're supposed to be the fastest man in the league?" he called after Mickey.

For all his Tiger spirit, Billy missed playing on the same team with his Yankee buddies. Yankee Stadium seemed like home, not Tiger Stadium. Early in the season, when the Tigers played in New York, Billy walked into the Stadium and stopped off at the switchboard to say hello to the elderly operator. She leaped out of her seat and took Billy's hand in both of hers. "*My* Billy Martin," she cried out.

"I'm sorry I don't have any fruit," he said, speaking of his former practice of buying her something from a fruit stand on his way to the Stadium. "I came straight from the hotel in a cab."

"Go on now, Billy," the woman simpered. "Don't be sorry."

As Billy walked away, the operator said, "What a sweet boy."

During pregame practice Billy asked a reporter to take a message into the Yankee clubhouse for Mickey Mantle, saying where he would meet him after the game. Martin explained that he didn't want to socialize too much on the field with Mickey. "There's a no-fraternizing rule," he said. Few players have ever worried about that rule. Martin's real reason was that Mantle might have trouble with the Yankee front office if he was seen talking with Martin.

The year with Detroit did not go well. Manager Jack Tighe lost his job in mid-season. Billy batted .255 and failed to ignite his teammates. Detroit finished fifth.

Over the winter Cleveland traded their two key bullpen

pitchers to Detroit for Martin, demonstrating that his value in trades was still high. Cleveland General Manager Frank Lane thought the spark that didn't ignite the Tigers would work on the Indians. Besides, Billy would be switched back to his normal position, second base. Lane said he was weary of watching ground balls roll by Bobby Avila, the current Indian second baseman.

In spring training with Cleveland, Martin was asked about reports that the Tigers had improved. "Them, improved?" he said, scraping the mud off his spikes after a game. "How can you improve a bunch of spoiled babies? If they get too mean this season I might take away their diapers. The trouble with them is they got too much publicity, too much money, and not enough spirit."

Billy put down his shoes and spoke about his season at Detroit. He was bitter. "When I got there," he said, "I was told these guys didn't play as a team. I was told to fire them up in spring training. I talked so much about the pennant, I got to believe it myself. But you see what Al Kaline said about me the other day: 'We don't have that pop-off Martin talking about pennants.' I say if you don't talk about winning a pennant and think it all the time, you don't belong in baseball. A leader can't lead that club, because they won't let you.

"The whole year in Detroit," Billy continued, "was a buildup to a letdown. With the Yankees I could move guys like Bauer, Woodling, and Mantle, but I couldn't do it to those guys. Every time you'd tell them something, somebody'd make a smart crack back at you."

The 1959 season in Cleveland, when Billy was thirty-one, did not live up to Billy's hopes and the Cleveland management's expectations. He played in only half of Cleveland's games, batting .260 with only 24 RBIs. His jaw was fractured by a pitch in August, but even when he recovered, manager Joe Gordon did not use him regularly. "We really had a winner for sure," Martin said later. "But Gordon blew it. Gordon didn't like me, but when he gave me the works, it cost him the pennant. He took me out of the lineup when we were moving and put me back too late. He let his personal feelings hurt the team."

The next stop on Billy's ride was Cincinnati, in the National League. This time he was one of three players sent to acquire one, second baseman Johnny Temple. In 103 games for the Reds, his batting average dropped to .246 and his RBI production to a mere 16. The only memorable event of the season was a fight he had with Jim Brewer, a rookie pitcher with the Chicago Cubs.

Brewer knocked Martin down with a brushback pitch. Billy flung his bat out toward the mound and walked out after it. Words were exchanged, then Billy threw a punch at Brewer, three inches taller and twenty pounds heavier than Martin. "That was the only time in my life I threw the first punch, and he had his arm cocked," Billy claimed. Martin's teammates rushed over for a brief melee. Afterward, Brewer was taken to the hospital with a broken orbital bone in his eye. He was out the rest of the season, having to undergo two eye operations. Martin maintained that he hit Brewer on the chin and that it was Billy's roommate, Cal McLish, who later hit Brewer in the eye. The National League office fined Martin $500 and suspended him for five days.

In September the Chicago Cubs and Jim Brewer jointly sued Billy Martin and the Reds for more than a million dollars. "Cash or check?" Billy cracked. But he knew he was in serious trouble.

"You'd think any guy who starts a fight would have the guts not to cry about it after he's hurt," Billy said about the suit. "Brewer had it coming to him. He's a real troublemaker."

It was Billy the Kid, however, who had the reputation as a troublemaker. And now, many viewed him as a dangerous, maiming psychotic. None of his previous fights had resulted in damage that hurt a player's career. This one did. And before, his reputation as a brawler had been balanced by his reputation as a winner. He was no longer a winner. Eventually Martin had to pay $22,500 to settle the suit. He couldn't pay anything to restore his reputation.

Martin's next stop on his trail of trades, in 1961, was with the Milwaukee Braves. This time no players were offered for him—only cash, and not very much. Billy desperately wanted to make this team, which had finished first or second for the last six years. "I don't want any more losers," he said in spring training. "I want one more winner." Then the Braves acquired Frank Bolling to play second for them before the season started. "They made a big deal to get Bolling," Billy said. "But I'm not checking out of the fight. I never worked harder to get in shape and I will get the chance. I will get it and I'll be ready."

He appeared in only six games with the Braves, all as a pinch hitter, before he was traded on June 1. The Minnesota Twins landed him by sending the Braves a minor-league infielder and a small amount of money. Billy played regularly at second for the Twins, appearing in more games than he had since Detroit. His .246 average equaled his career low, and his 17 errors were more than he had ever made in a Yankee season. His reflexes had slowed.

The Twins released Billy Martin from the team during spring training of 1962, ending his eleven-year major-league career not long before his thirty-fourth birthday. Martin was offered $100,000 to play in Japan. He turned it down, deciding it was more important for him to stay in American baseball. His reputation was at its lowest, but baseball was the only world he had ever known and the only future he wanted. In the long run he couldn't afford to disappear to Japan, no matter how much money he could make there in the short term.

"I had been knocked down so badly," he said. "The things they said about me. And when I was released, I was determined to come back. I thought, I got to stay in this game. I was going to eat humble pie, but I had to prove to people in baseball that I was a different person than who they thought I was. I'd let them see the real Billy Martin. But some of the stuff would follow me wherever I went."

Martin signed on with the Twins as a $10,000-a-year "troubleshooter," actually a scout, the lowest rung of the ladder in a baseball organization.

Martin once summed up his post-Yankee career as a player. "I was still a Yankee," he said. "I tried to play baseball as I'd been taught, and I found it hard. I talked and acted with the self-assurance of the Yankees and discovered that a few of my teammates resented it. And, in my heart, I thought: 'How I miss Casey and the Yanks.'"

Chapter 11
FRUITS OF A LONG APPRENTICESHIP

Billy Martin brags that he makes moves other managers are scared to make. Against all tradition, he may order a left-handed pitcher to walk a lefty batter in order to get at a right-handed hitter. Most managers are too afraid of second-guessing to go against "The Book"—that unpublished tome of conventional baseball wisdom. Whatever else they think of him, baseball people respect Martin for his daring, originality, and intelligence as a manager.

"Gene Mauch and Billy Martin are the two best strategists in the game," said Al Campanis, vice-president of the Los Angeles Dodgers. "They're both like Prussian generals."

Asked in the middle of the '76 season why the Yankees were winning, Chuck Tanner, manager of the Oakland A's, said, "One reason: Billy Martin."

Earl Weaver, manager of the Baltimore Orioles, summed it up in his own impish style. "Billy Martin is the smartest man ever to get fired by three clubs," he said.

The short, talkative Oriole skipper brings out Billy's

competitiveness more than does any other manager, mainly because Weaver has been the most successful manager
in the American League over the last decade. Ever since
Martin became manager of the Twins, in 1969, Earl and
Billy have engaged in a running feud, baiting each other
and exchanging put-downs. Earl explained the feud very
simply: "We have a burning desire to beat each other." At
the end of the '76 season, Earl said he believed Martin
should be chosen manager of the year. "He's only the second manager to have won more than one Eastern Division
title," Weaver said. Then he added, "I've won five."

Weaver has been reported to enjoy his drinks, and after
one drunken-driving incident that made the papers, Martin
sent Weaver a picture of a police car. Weaver retaliated by
mailing Billy a picture of a bathing beauty with Martin's
head pasted on it. The rivalry, though, hasn't always been
that humorous.

The Yankee-Oriole games in 1976 brought out Martin's
most imaginative managing and his most combative in-
stincts. In the eighth inning of the July 27 game in Baltimore, which the Orioles eventually won, Dock Ellis hit
Reggie Jackson in the face with a fastball. The Orioles
strongly suspected that the beaning was intentional. In the
ninth inning Jim Palmer, who does not like to throw at batters, felt it necessary to retaliate. When Mickey Rivers
came to bat, Palmer hit him on the shoulder—with one of
the slowest fastballs he threw all year.

"That was about the weakest knockdown I ever saw in
my life. It belongs in the Hall of Shame," Martin said after
the game. Still, he was angry—at Weaver rather than at
Palmer. "Knowing Jim, I'm sure he was directed to hit Rivers. He's not that type of guy," Billy said. "I'll deck Earl at
home plate the next time one of our guys is deliberately
thrown at."

Martin had showered by then and was putting on his
clothes. His T-shirt, with orange lettering across the chest,

read, I'M A FUCKING GENIUS. "That's Earl's shirt," Billy explained. "He don't need it no more."

Martin did not deck Earl Weaver in the next Oriole-Yan-
kee series, but Lou Piniella almost did, during an August 8
game at Yankee Stadium. One of baseball's best bench
jockeys, Weaver had made a practice of needling Piniella
while he was batting—usually by calling out to him what
pitch was coming. Lou, a cheerful but short-tempered player, didn't appreciate the help. In the fourth inning Piniella
charged toward the Oriole dugout, flinging his bat along
the ground in the direction of Weaver. Martin quickly
sprinted over to make sure that Lou didn't actually go into
the Baltimore dugout after Weaver.

"If it had been me," Billy said of Weaver after the game,
"I'd have had guts enough to come out of the dugout if a guy
threw a bat at me. He hid behind the bat rack. He backed
off in a womanly way. I didn't want Lou to beat up a little
midget like that. It wouldn't have looked good in the papers."

Weaver, whose team won the game, dismissed Martin's
criticism of his manhood. "I don't think Lou was really coming after me this time," Weaver said, "but you never know
when he'll snap. A few years ago, I would probably have
gone out after him—and gotten my ass whipped, too."

The needle Martin most enjoyed applying against Weaver was baseball strategy. During the September 5 game
against the Orioles, Billy made a very unusual move in the
sixth inning. With a runner at first and two out, Sandy Alomar, the starting second baseman replacing the injured
Willie Randolph, was scheduled to bat. He had been sick
with a virus, and Martin decided to take him out of the
game and replace him at second with César Tovar, the designated hitter. To hit for Alomar, Martin sent up the pitcher, Catfish Hunter, a fine hitter before the designated-
hitter rule idled American League pitchers' bats. Martin
explained to the umpire that since he was sending his des-

ignated hitter into the field, his pitcher would have to hit. The umpire okayed the move, and Earl Weaver did not protest it.

Billy Martin knows the rule book. Earlier in the year he had protested a game because a substitute outfielder took seven warmup throws instead of the five allowed by the rule book. Probably no other manager knew that rule, or would have been counting. And Billy Martin was probably the only one on the field, or in the stands, who knew he was violating a rule by having Hunter hit for Alomar. The rule stipulates that "the game pitcher may only pinch hit for the designated hitter," which in this case would have been Tovar, not Alomar.

Since Hunter grounded out and the Yankees lost the game, the move couldn't be called successful. It did, however, give Martin a score over Weaver in their rivalry. After the game, Billy explained, "I knew what the rule was. It was an illegal move and I knew it. I was just trying to see if I could get away with something. I told the guys on the bench I don't think I can do this, but I'm going to try it. If they had told me I couldn't do it, then I would've put Otto Velez up, but I wanted to save Velez for later.

"I was surprised Weaver didn't protest," Billy added with a smile. "I can't fault the umpire. When the hell did you ever see anyone do it? The guy who looks bad is Earl. All he had to do was protest."

No manager has studied the rule book or any other aspect of baseball longer or harder than has Billy Martin. Lacking great natural skills, he learned early to rely on his brains as a player. Back in 1948, in the minor leagues, Martin found a mentor in Casey Stengel, and he began serving a long apprenticeship to become a manager.

"I don't suspect I'll ever be asked to manage a team," Yankee second baseman Billy Martin told a writer in 1956.

Martin acted as the Yankees' team leader and Casey Stengel treated him as an apprentice manager, spending time with Billy on the bench explaining strategies. But Martin thought even back then that his reputation would frustrate his ambition to manage.

Others thought differently. Roger Kahn, author of *The Boys of Summer* and long an acute observer of baseball, predicted in *Sport* in 1957, after Martin had been traded by the Yankees, that the cocky second baseman would eventually become a manager.

At the tail end of his playing career Billy knew more than ever what he was up against. While waiting to be sold or traded by the Braves in the spring of 1961, he asked a reporter, "Do you think some day I'll get the chance to be a manager?" Then he answered his own question. "I don't think so, because I've got the reputation for being baseball's bad boy, and I don't deserve that reputation.

"If I don't get the chance to manage it would be a big mistake," he continued. "I could do a good job. If I can lead men as a player, why wouldn't they follow me as a manager? I know how to handle men. That's the secret of managing. For another, I know enough about the game, not just fundamentals but executing. I think I could get the most out of players with common sense and psychology. I'm fiery enough and I'd have their respect. Unfortunately, I don't think I'll ever get the chance, and there's nothing in the world can change that."

By the time Billy entered the Minnesota organization, he had all but given up on the idea of managing. He just wanted a job that would keep him in baseball. And he wanted some stability in his life, after five years of migrant work in the fields of baseball.

In 1959, after his season in Cleveland, Billy had made one choice for stability. He married Gretchen Winkler, a former airline stewardess from Nebraska. Gretchen understood Billy and his devotion to baseball. "He brings the

game home," she said. "Anybody who doesn't is a terrific ac-
tor or he really doesn't care." "She's the one who gets mad
all the time around the house," Billy said of his wife. "But
she's a very level-headed, intelligent woman, and a very
pretty one. I couldn't have picked a better girl."

In his first year as Minnesota scout Billy and Gretchen
bought their first house, in suburban Richfield, near the
Twins' park. In their backyard they grew eggplant and to-
matoes, and Billy worked around the house and garden.
"He's one of those people who just has to be doing something all the time," said Gretchen.

Calvin Griffith, the president and owner of the Twins,
had taken a fancy to Billy and had encouraged him to enter
the organization after his release as a player. He assured
Martin that he had a long-term career with the Minnesota
organization. After Martin dutifully served as a scout for
three years, Griffith brought him up to the Twins as third-
base coach.

In 1965, his first year coaching, the Twins went from
sixth place to the pennant. Part of the credit for the turn-
about went to Billy Martin. Billy took a special interest in
the Twins' moody shortstop, Zoilo Versalles. Martin decided that the way to help Versalles develop his potential was
by giving him hell, but carefully, always away from the
other players so that his pride would not be offended. Billy
coaxed the small infielder into becoming more aggressive at
the plate, releasing the ball quicker in the field, and using
his speed more on the bases. At the end of the '65 season,
Versalles won the Most Valuable Player award in the
American League. Martin also devoted time to developing
another Latin-American infielder, César Tovar.

Minnesota manager Sam Mele thought Martin had done
an excellent job and was enthusiastic about Billy's returning for the 1966 season. That enthusiasm was not shared by
Martin's fellow coaches, Jim Lemon, Hal Naragon, and
Johnny Sain. The three of them hung around together and

were antagonistic toward Billy. Sain almost didn't return for the '66 season because of his antipathy toward Martin. The third-base coach's take-charge style apparently did not mesh well with that of his peers.

Billy also had trouble with a key member of the Minnesota organization, traveling secretary Howard Fox. Bad feelings between the two finally boiled over during a July road trip in the 1966 season. After losing three straight games to the Yankees in Minnesota, the Twins shared a charter flight with their rivals. The plane was to carry the Twins to Washington and then fly on up to New York with the Yankees. Scheduled to take off at nine P.M., the plane didn't make it off the ground until after midnight. The players and coaches, including Martin, passed the time where they usually pass time waiting for flights—in the airport cocktail lounge.

On the plane several of the Yankees exchanged heated words with a steward who ordered the liquor service to be cut off. Howard Fox suggested to Martin that he have a word with the boisterous Yankees, since many of them were Martin's friends and ex-teammates. Billy refused, saying it was none of his business. On the bus from Dulles International Airport, Martin and Fox argued loudly in front of the Twins and many of their wives who happened to be along on this road trip. "He just kept egging me on," Fox said later. "I was getting pretty mad." It was five in the morning by the time the team arrived at the Statler-Hilton in Washington. One of the traveling secretary's jobs was to pass out the room keys in the lobby. Fox kept Martin waiting until last to get his key, then flung it at him.

"One day I'm going to take you outside and beat the living hell out of you," Billy yelled at him. Fox, eight years older than Martin but well built, took off his glasses and yelled back, "How about here, right now!" The fight didn't last long and it did not go well for the traveling secretary.

Late the next morning, Billy was worried. Someone told

him that Fox, who was wearing a black eye, had told Griffith to choose between Martin and Fox. That would be bad news, Billy knew, because Howard happened to be one of Griffith's best friends. Fox, however, denied having made any such ultimatum. Griffith called a meeting when the team reached Boston four days later. After presiding over a morning-long session with manager Sam Mele and the full coaching staff, he announced that Martin was being fined $100 for "using mild invectives" while women were aboard the bus from the airport. In his statement Griffith passed over the fight itself, saying he had to do more research. He announced, "Both Fox and Martin shook hands here today, and the incident is over and forgotten." But neither man forgot.

Despite the ruckus, rumors began to surface late in the '66 season that Martin was being considered for managing jobs. The Red Sox and the Tigers were both reported to be interested in him. Martin did not respond with any enthusiasm about the prospect of managing. "Look, I'm in no hurry to manage," he said. "I don't want to rush into a bad job. Too many guys take the first shot they get in the major leagues, and if they flop because of a weak organization, they never get a second chance. When you make the move, you've got to be sure it's in a stable organization with a team that has a chance to win."

Martin had settled into his coaching job. He had convinced himself that he was happy with what he was doing, and that he really didn't want to think about managing. "I was perfectly content to remain as third-base coach just the way Frank Crosetti did with the Yankees under a succession of managers," he said later. Billy stayed on as Twins third-base coach through 1967 and into the 1968 season.

Then, in late May, a delegation came to meet with Cal Griffith from the Twins' Triple-A farm club in Denver. A change of managers was needed, they said, and they suggested Billy Martin. Griffith said that he didn't think Martin would be interested in the job but that he would ask him.

Griffith was encouraged by some of his front office to send Billy to Denver. It would put the troublesome coach out of the way, and since they believed he would probably handle the team badly, the anti-Martin faction would then have an excuse to push him out of the Twins' organization entirely.

When Griffith offered Billy the job, Martin was surprised. And he was unsure. Once before, in the minor leagues at Oakland prior to joining the Yankees, Martin had not welcomed a chance to advance himself. Then as a Coast League player, now as a major-league coach, Billy felt he had achieved a level of security and had deep doubts about taking the next step up the ladder. "I didn't want to go," he said. "I was happy doing what I was doing."

That night, when he told Gretchen about the offer, she urged him to accept it. "I could see how frustrated he was. I told him he had to go to Denver to prove he could manage. I knew he wouldn't be happy if he didn't try it," she said. Billy and Gretchen stayed up until one in the morning discussing it. "I couldn't sleep that night," Billy recalled. "Then the next morning, I surprised myself by accepting."

Billy took over a demoralized Denver team with an 8–22 record. The first thing he did was impose discipline, beginning with dress standards. Turtlenecks would no longer be acceptable for public appearances. All players would have to wear shirts with ties and jackets. "I told them I didn't mind long sideburns and long hair, but they would have to keep them neat," Billy said. "It's a little thing, but pride starts with little things. I wanted us to look like gentlemen, not hippies."

This did not mean Billy was transforming himself into a stuffy, establishment type of manager. On the contrary, he was at his most fiery and flamboyant. "I had a tendency to yell more," he said recently about his Denver days. "I got upset more, trying to prove myself." His temper, directed at umpires, resulted in his being thrown out of 8 of the team's remaining 115 games. The team made a total turnaround under Martin, winning 65 of those 115. Billy Martin had succeeded in his new challenge. Once again, he had proved himself.

Meanwhile, the Twins, who had come within a game of winning the pennant in 1967, dropped to seventh place in 1968. Manager Carl Ermer was fired. The Twins had played sluggishly and Ermer had lost control of the team, which had divided into cliques based on ethnic backgrounds. The Denver manager, Griffith was aware, had not only proved he could turn a losing team around; he also had the reputation for establishing rapport with black and Latin-American players. "I'm from a minority, too," Martin once explained. "I grew up like they grew up. When nothing and nothing are talking to each other, they understand each other."

At a news conference on October 11, 1968, Calvin Griffith stood next to a smiling Billy Martin and announced the new manager of the Twins. "You people in the news media certainly helped the decision," Griffith said to the reporters. "I'd never seen such a campaign in my life about one personality. I feel that Billy has the ability to be another Casey Stengel. Of course, my brother-in-law says that Billy's either going to be the greatest manager in baseball or the worst," Griffith added, referring to Sherry Robertson, who ran the Twins' farm system.

Martin, with emotion in his voice, called the appointment "a dream, a challenge . . . the kind of challenge I've always loved, and one which I'm sure will bring the best out of me and my ballclub."

After the news conference, Griffith revealed second thoughts about his selection of Martin, telling one reporter he felt as if he were sitting on a keg of dynamite. A few months later, the Twins' owner spoke with Minneapolis

Tribune sports columnist Sid Hartman about the hiring of Martin. "There wasn't ever any question in my mind that he knew baseball," Griffith said of Martin. "But I never felt that he would be able to control himself enough to be the Twins' manager. When Billy decided to take the Denver job last year, I had a long talk with him. I pointed out some of his weaknesses and strengths. I honestly thought his temperament would be a problem. I never promised him he would manage the Twins. I did suggest that he would get a better job in our organization if he was successful at Denver.

"The only thing I ever knew about Martin's off-the-field activities was what I had read in the paper," Griffith continued. "He didn't have the best reputation. Before he went to Denver, Billy assured me that a lot of the off-field problems weren't his fault. Martin has never lied to me, so I believed him. The job he did at Denver was amazing."

Griffith's comments did not add up to a ringing endorsement of Martin. Enough doubts showed through in the interview that if Billy were a cautious man, he would have played it very carefully as rookie manager. Billy Martin is not a cautious man.

His daring, aggressive style on the field could be seen early in spring training. In one game, Martin faced another rookie manager, Ted Williams, who had just taken over the Washington Senators. With two outs and the score tied in the seventh the Twins had the bases loaded, and Martin flashed the squeeze sign. The daring gambit worked perfectly, with the bunter winding up on first and the runner scoring from third. "Well, you should have seen Ted Williams and some of the Senators," Martin recounted the day after. "You'd have thought I committed murder. They were calling me everything. While this was going on, our runner on third stole home to put us two runs in front. Williams was blowing his stack by now. I don't know what he was thinking or saying. I didn't care. I wasn't trying to show him up. I wanted those two runs. I wanted to win the game."

No game is meaningless to Billy. And the fact that Ted Williams was receiving more spring publicity than Martin was a goad to the Minnesota manager. Martin seemed intent on provoking a feud with Williams. "He was the greatest hitter I ever saw," he told one reporter, "but as a second baseman, I didn't have any respect for him, because he never slid into me. On a double play he'd go out of the baselines. It's nothing personal."

Martin had quickly established his managerial style with his running game and his running mouth, both of which produced spectacular results during the season. The Twins had been a conservative, hard-hitting club—they had some of the best hitters in the league in Harmon Killebrew, Rod Carew, and Tony Oliva. But Billy wanted them to run, too, something they had not previously done. Before the season was half over, the Twins had stolen home eight times, Carew already tying the American League record with six steals. "I've always said home is the easiest base to steal, if you time it right," Billy said of the game's rarest and most exciting offensive play. "You can get a big lead, because you know the pitcher is taking a windup." By midseason pitchers stopped taking windups when a Twin was on third. While that almost eliminated Minnesota's opportunities to steal home, it also limited the pitcher. Anyway, the Twins were busy stealing other bases. Even sluggish slugger Killebrew, who had stolen seven bases in the previous fifteen seasons, had four by mid-season.

Billy's running mouth caused a stir for the first time on May 18. After four straight losses, Martin was in a bad temper. And as he often does in a bad temper, he shot his mouth off. He didn't speak of the losing streak; instead, speaking to reporters in the clubhouse, he blasted the Twins' farm-system chiefs. Martin was angry because he and Griffith had agreed to send a rookie pitcher, Charlie Walters, down from the Twins to Denver. Then, after Martin had told Walters he was ticketed for Denver, Walters was instead sent to a Double-A club, one step further down the ladder.

The Twins' farm director was Sherry Robertson, Calvin's brother-in-law. Martin aimed most of his fire at assistant farm director George Brophy. "I may be old-fashioned," Billy said, "but I thought that when you went from the big leagues, you go to Triple-A. How in the hell am I supposed to tell something like that to Walters? Brophy said he hasn't got a curveball. The kid's been working on it, and for the last six days he's thrown one helluva curveball. But Brophy never goes out on the field. How could he know?"

Martin was asked where he was going to use Walters' replacement, Jerry Crider. "I don't know yet if he'll start or relieve," Martin said with scorn. "I'll have to clear it with Brophy."

Martin said he wasn't criticizing Griffith himself. "But he gets all kinds of alibis and lies," Martin said. "These are my players. I didn't sign them. I inherited them. But I'm going to fight for them. This manager is no figurehead. If we're going to lose, it will be my way and nobody else's. I know managers get fired, but let me die my way."

When Brophy was reached by reporters, his only comment was a reminder that Martin had broken protocol. "Billy and I have worked together for eight years now, and I'm sure he'll feel differently in the morning," he said. "Even if I were to reply to some of these things, the newspapers aren't the place." For his part, Sherry Robertson said that Martin was "totally out of line. I don't tell Martin how to manage his team. I don't need him to tell me how to run the farm department. Brophy and I will handle player development. Martin should stick to managing."

The next day, Griffith called a meeting of his brother-in-law, his assistant farm director, and his manager. After twenty-five minutes, a somber Martin came out and announced, "I should have said what I did to them personally and not gone through the papers. I've apologized to both Sherry and Brophy and I hope it's forgotten." Once again, though, Martin could not forget. Sometime later he commented about George Brophy, "If he'd been a younger man, I'd have punched his lights out."

Frank Lane, a general manager at Cleveland who once traded for Billy and once traded him away, has said, "When I've talked like he does, I've always made sure I was talking on a five-year or seven-year contract." Martin was on a one-year contract.

Discretion has never been Billy Martin's style. Early in the '69 season a reporter began a radio interview with the Minnesota manager by saying, "President Nixon said that he thinks Baltimore or Chicago will win the pennant." Most managers would have politely muttered how the president is certainly a fine baseball fan and has a right to his opinion. Martin said, "I don't think he's very good at predictions. I remember when he predicted he would be elected Governor of California. He hasn't made it yet."

Perhaps to demonstrate his nonpartisanship, Martin also took on Hubert Humphrey. The recently defeated presidential candidate was brought into the Minnesota clubhouse on Griffith's request for a picture-taking session. It was just after a tough loss, and Martin told Griffith, "I don't care who he is. No picture-taking in *my* clubhouse." Humphrey was understanding, but Griffith was not. "Nobody short of the pope would get in," Billy explained later, according to one report, "and maybe not even him. I'd probably try to explain, 'Your Holiness, I'm sorry, but these one-run games . . .'"

In case Griffith missed the point about the clubhouse being Billy's domain, he also barred Calvin's grown son from the clubhouse. Billy thought young Griffith was telling the players too much about his daddy's opinion of them.

Meanwhile, the Twins played exciting baseball, drew more fans, and won games. Martin was succeeding, mainly by demanding the best out of his players. "A lot of veterans don't like to be told about little things," said Frank Quilici, utility infielder. "They figure they've been around and they know when they do something wrong. But Billy believes in telling them anyway." Martin did not hesitate to chew out any player, veteran or rookie. "The day after he chews you out," Quilici added, "he'll sit down and talk it out with you, explain it, and you'll know where you stand. And he'll play you again in the same situation."

"Playing for Martin is not the easiest job in the world," said catcher John Roseboro, "because he wants everything just so. But as long as you're winning, you don't give a damn how hard it is."

Martin's most interesting relationship with a player was with pitcher Dave Boswell. A starting pitcher coming off a 10–13 season in 1968, Dave was just as hot-tempered and fiery as his manager, and he often exploded at his team-mates when he thought they had let him down. Dave always hated to be taken out of a game. Once, though, in June, Billy went out to the mound and asked him if he was tired. Dave admitted he was, so Billy lifted him. Later Dave told his manager, "You know, you're the first man I've ever told the truth to." That pleased Martin a great deal.

Boswell was having trouble with the middle finger of his pitching hand—it blistered after six or seven innings. He asked Martin for advice. Billy suggested soaking it in pickle brine, a cure he once used for blisters. "It worked wonders for my fingers," Billy said, then added, "but my legs went bad." The pickle brine had toughened Boswell's hands by the time of his most famous encounter with Martin, on August 6 at the Lindell AC in Detroit. Billy said later that if he had known some of his players were in the bar, he would not have gone in. On this night Dave and his team-mate Bob Allison had a few too many. After Martin arrived the players began arguing. Soon they went outside and Boswell began throwing punches. Martin followed them outside and tried to intervene. Boswell, six-three and 190 pounds, swung at his 160-pound manager. According to Martin's account, "He hit me in the temple and the ribs. I just held on, and then I started to hit him in the stomach. I worked up and hit him in the mouth, nose, and eyes. He bounced off the wall, and I hit him again, and he was out cold before he hit the ground."

When Martin's punches exploded into the newspapers the next day, they did not please owner Cal Griffith. He did not like the idea of his manager drinking with the players, much less fighting with them. Boswell, however, held no grudges. And the punches didn't hurt his pitching. He went on to win twenty games, for the first and only time in his career. As soon as he delivered the final pitch of his twentieth win, Dave ran into the dugout, grabbed his manager, and kissed him on the forehead. "He went flaky for a minute," Billy explained with a grin.

All the excitement that Martin stirred up on the Twins seemed to have worked. With a 97–65 record, the team finished first in the Western Division—it was the first year the league was divided into divisions. The Twins lost the first American League championship series in three straight games to the Orioles, who had overpowered the Eastern Division with a 109–53 record. The playoffs were closer than the 3–0 record indicated, however, since the first two games went into extra innings before the Twins lost. In all, it had been a fine year for the Twins and their rookie manager.

At the end of the playoffs Griffith called Martin into his office for a conference. Billy assumed it would be about his new contract, and he had a few ideas in mind. For one, he wanted more money; second, he wanted a two-year contract; third, he wanted a clearer line of authority.

Griffith said to him, "I just can't make up my mind about anything."

"What?" Martin replied. Then the meaning sunk in. Griffith, the paternalistic owner who had taken such interest in Martin, was preparing to dump him.

"I want to spell out one thing before I leave this room," Billy said to him. "Did I do everything I said I was going to do?"

Griffith said, "Yes."

"Did I make them hustle?"

"Yes."

"Did they *win?*"

"Yes."

Then Billy zeroed in on what he believed was the real trouble—his nemesis, Howard Fox, who had been criticizing Martin to the players as well as to the front office.

"Did you stop Mr. Fox from talking about me to the players like he did?" Martin asked the owner.

"I told him to," Griffith said.

"You didn't stop him," Martin said. "I did my end. You didn't do yours. You do whatever you want to. And I still have the utmost respect for you."

Billy Martin walked out of the office and told reporters he considered himself "out of work." Billy went duck hunting, and Griffith went to the World Series in New York. At ten o'clock Monday morning Calvin Griffith called Billy to tell him, "I have some bad news for you." Billy had already heard the bad news on the radio Sunday night.

In announcing the firing to the press, Griffith said that Martin "didn't want to come in and see me. He thought I was being critical of the ballplayers. I never told him how to play the game of baseball. I never interfered with him doing his job on the field. But I think the Twins are as much a part of me as of Billy Martin."

Anticipating the public reaction to the firing, Griffith added, "You know, Billy can go into a crowd and charm the hell out of you. But," he said, almost plaintively, "he ignored me."

As Griffith expected, Minnesota fans were outraged. All

day the switchboard buzzed with calls from season-ticket holders. "Some of the callers are leaving their names and saying to take them off the season-ticket list," said the switchboard operator. "All of them are mad, and some of them are downright dirty."

Griffith, feeling on the defensive, elaborated on his reasons for firing Martin. He told one reporter, "There are certain things I don't want to get into." Then he got into them. "For instance, some people wrote in the paper about the card-playing among the players. One thing I won't tolerate is gambling on the club." Griffith implied that Martin himself had participated in the card games—and he had.

"They've been doing it for a hundred years," Martin retorted. "The way I looked at it was, how was he finding these things out? Howard Fox is telling him. If he's going to fire me, fire me! Don't come up with pettiness. Little childish things. If it wasn't playing cards, I might have taken a cold shower. Didn't shower in my room, showered with the players. And that's too much communication. I was fired for overcommunicating, and other managers have been fired for undercommunicating. Whatever the excuse is, they're going to be looking for it. Who's kidding who?"

Martin summed up his feelings. "I was disenchanted. Very disenchanted."

For the first time in his adult life Billy Martin was out of baseball. And he remained out for a year, missing the 1970 season. He kept busy, appearing regularly on two early-morning radio shows in Minneapolis and working as a special assistant to the president of the station. He also worked for Grain Belt Breweries, in the public relations department, speaking at clinics and luncheons. And he helped Bob Short, owner of the Washington Senators, in his unsuccessful campaign for the Democratic nomination for governor of Minnesota.

Billy later called 1970 "the loneliest year of my life."

Chapter 12
LONG-TERM CONTRACTS

The Yankees arrived at the last week of August, 1976, enjoying a 9½-game lead in the Eastern Division—and Billy Martin still did not have a new contract. When asked about it, principal owner George Steinbrenner said, "Between the lines, Billy Martin is the best manager in the game." Some sportswriters took that to be an unqualified endorsement of Martin, indicating a new contract was imminent. But the words were probably not so soothing to Martin's ears. Curiously, they echoed the words Jim Campbell, general manager of the Detroit Tigers, had used when he fired Martin in 1973: "From foul line to foul line, Billy has done a good job."

When the Yankees reached September with an 11½-game lead, Steinbrenner at last became convinced that the team would not fold. He assured everyone that Martin would be offered a new contract, and he sat down to negotiate with Billy. Steinbrenner offered a two-year contract. Martin was adamant about a three-year contract. Steinbrenner would not budge from his offer, and Billy decided to wait him out.

On September 9 Steinbrenner called Martin into his plush office in Yankee Stadium. When Billy walked in, he saw his old contract lying on the owner's desk. "Well, how about it?" Billy asked. Steinbrenner pulled out a new contract—for three years. In it Martin's responsibilities and duties were clearly spelled out, something both Billy and his boss had wanted. For the 1976 season Martin was being paid $75,000. The dollar figures on the new contract had been left blank. "You fill in the numbers," Martin said to Steinbrenner. The principal owner filled in more than $300,000 for the three years, in salary and living expenses. "He was very fair," Billy later said about the money.

The new contract was announced on September 12, just before the Saturday-afternoon game. "George was being real cute, bringing Dick Williams into the Stadium and all," Martin said after the announcement. "But I never ran scared in my life. I didn't push, even though I wondered. Look, I was holding the hammer. Then we ran off more wins, and the hammer was stronger than ever."

Steinbrenner was asked if he felt put on the spot by Martin's insistence on three years. "No," he said. "Billy and I have a rapport that few people in sports have. I've seen him go to Minnesota and Detroit and Texas and do a hell of a job and get fired. I don't think that will happen here, because I know Billy. I know how to get along with him. We joke with each other—I tell him he's number one and a half, I'm number one—but he knows he has to go along with the system.

"In a winning organization, no one is indispensable," the Yankees' "number one" continued. "That goes for the manager and it goes for me, too, and I think Billy understands that now."

Billy admitted that the three years meant a great deal to him. "I wanted it for security and as a matter of pride," he said. "Three other clubs fired me, then went around bad-mouthing me. It's a matter of pride that after what they all said about me, somebody was willing to give me a three-year contract. And I'm determined to prove it was no mistake."

He then went out and lost a 6–5 game to Detroit, the second of the three clubs that fired him.

The year Billy Martin was out of baseball, 1970, was also the year one of his former teams fell apart. Jim Campbell, general manager of the Detroit Tigers, was desperate by the end of the season, just two years after the Tigers had won the World Series. Their superpitcher, Denny McLain, who had won 55 games and two Cy Young awards in '68 and '69, had been suspended from baseball for the beginning of the '70 season—for involvement in a bookie operation. When he returned, on July 1, he had turned into a mediocre pitcher, at best. Catcher Bill Freehan's diary of the '69 season had been published and had caused hard feelings among a number of players. Everyone was unhappy with everyone else. There was no communication between the players and manager Mayo Smith, no communication between the players and coaches, and little communication among the players.

"This club was a disgrace," said one player after the season. "We were accepting money under false pretenses."

"People who paid their way into our games were being gypped." said another.

Detroit finished in fourth place in the Eastern Division, 29 games behind the Orioles. Before the season ended, Campbell met with Billy Martin to discuss his becoming manager of the Tigers. It was a surprising choice of manager for the conservative, image-minded baseball executive. But Campbell knew he needed a tough man to take charge of the team, one who could rekindle a championship spirit. And Martin was that kind of man.

Billy had already had some feelers from other ballclubs during his year out of baseball. He had been burned once, though, and he was anxious to return to the game on his own terms. In his rookie season as a manager he had proved himself to be a winner, so he knew he had a bargaining position. He liked Campbell's offer. Detroit was a potential pennant winner. Perhaps, also, the irony appealed to Martin—returning to a team that had traded him away a dozen years before.

During their discussions Campbell never once brought up the subject of Martin's temper. "What am I going to do, hire a man for what he is, and then try to change him? I think it's definitely one of his assets," Campbell said. "I really do. It's like anything else—you have to keep it under control. But Billy knows that."

For his part, Billy has never been apologetic for having a temper. "It seems to me Jesus Christ had a temper," Martin has said. "Didn't he whip the money changers and drive them out of the temple?"

After signing a contract for $65,000, Martin made it his first priority to meet with all the players individually during the off-season. He traveled to the homes of those who did not live in the Detroit area—to Massachusetts, California, Mexico. He spent time at a Detroit hotel, meeting with the players who lived nearby. He listened to them tell him what they thought was wrong on the club, why it was demoralized. He told them about pride, about hustling, and he said that all players would be treated alike. By that time, the player who had demanded and received the most special treatment, Denny McLain, had been traded away. One source of friction on the team had been eliminated. After his visits, Martin concluded, "This was a very unhappy club. It wasn't really anybody's fault—just a hell of a lot of people's fault."

When he arrived for spring training, Martin said, "The greatest asset I got going for me is communication with the players. There'll be no gap." Before his players took the field on the first day of training, the new manager called them together for a few words. "I am the leader," he announced. "When I see something wrong out there, I *will* comment on the bench, and I do get mad, and I am not a good loser, and I say if anybody in this room thinks I am a good loser, they're kidding themselves. I am a very, very bad loser. I've never heard there was such a thing as a good loser. I think that winning is the ultimate, but I'm not a crybaby. I'm going to lose at times, and I accept it as a man. But that doesn't mean I enjoy it. Because when I lose, it takes something out of me, and sometimes I can't eat dinner or get to sleep."

Casey Stengel was on hand a few days later to welcome his student back into the ranks of managers. "You better do what he says or he'll knock you on your butt," Casey said to all Tigers who happened to be in the vicinity.

During spring-training games Martin had his Tigers bunting and running, despite the fact the team was much slower and older than the average team. More important, he had them hustling. They kept hustling into the early weeks of the season. By mid-June, it became clear that the new manager had made the Tigers into a Billy Martin team.

During a game with the Indians in Cleveland, Detroit relief pitcher Bill Denehy hit Cleveland catcher Ray Fosse in the ribs with a pitch. Fosse charged to the mound and threw a body block on Denehy, who responded by kicking Fosse's hand. The burliest of all the Tigers, left fielder Willie Horton, who had been hit by a Cleveland pitcher earlier, didn't want to miss out on the action. He charged in from the outfield, slamming into the Indians and Tigers converging near the mound. It was a first-rate donnybrook, not the usual baseball shoving match, and the Tigers were clearly winning the fight by the time the peacemakers cooled the players down.

Martin was one of the peacemakers, wading through the tumbling players, arms outspread, calling for an end to the strife. Martin's Tigers, acting like tigers, had no need for his fists. Besides, one of his players could be hurt if the battle went on too long. After the game Martin openly deplored the violence. Later, however, he admitted, "I'm proud of the way my boys hung in there together. This was a very unhappy club a year ago. Now we're a team, a happy team."

Although Balitmore was heavily favored to repeat as Eastern Division champion, the Tigers kept within striking distance much of the season, with good pitching, power hitting and fiery managing. Mickey Lolich pitched every fourth day and ended up with a 25–14 record. The Tigers led the majors in home runs. And Martin was kicked out of 4 of the first 60 games, before he settled down for no ejections in the last 102 games.

In September Detroit made its run. Having been 7½ games behind Baltimore at the All-Star break, on September 18 the Tigers closed to within five games by beating the Orioles five straight times. But it was too late. Baltimore won their last eleven games and the division championship. Detroit finished in second place with an 91–71 record. Martin had brought his veteran team back from mediocrity to the fourth-best won-lost record in the major leagues.

In 1972 no "youth movement" surfaced to rejuvenate the team. Martin had to go with mostly the same veterans, now one year older. Nobody expected them to knock off the Orioles—nobody but Martin and the players he had managed to convince.

Martin was at his feistiest all season. One target for his agitation was Cleveland pitcher Gaylord Perry, who had just entered the league after years with the San Francisco Giants. Gaylord's brother, Jim, had pitched for Martin at Minnesota, and Martin knew Gaylord's best pitch was an illegal one. He had switched recently to a greaseball, after years of throwing a spitball. "I'm waiting to see that wet garbage," Martin warned Gaylord early in the season. "I'm waiting to see the cheating brother put on his act." American League president Joe Cronin had issued a directive that an opposing manager could demand that the umpire inspect a pitcher the manager suspected of concealing an "illegal substance." Billy intended to make full use of that directive.

In mid-May Perry had already won six games when he faced the Tigers at Detroit. Early in the game Martin came out to speak with plate umpire Lou DiMuro. The umpire then walked to the mound and said to Perry apologetically, "Martin wants me to feel your hair."

"Do I have to take off my cap?" the pitcher asked.

"Sorry," DiMuro said. Gaylord removed his cap, exposing his baldness to the delighted Detroit fans.

Later in the year Billy brought a bloodhound to the ballpark. He announced that the hound had been trained to sniff out Vaseline, which Martin suspected (and Perry later admitted) was the pitcher's favored grease. "Cronin won't believe me, but he might believe my dog," Martin said. The hound never made his appearance on the field to sniff at Perry, but the publicity made the point for Billy. No dog or umpire, however, ever succeeded in finding where Perry kept his supply of grease. And Martin complained all year long about the inability of the umpire and of Cronin to stop Perry's flouting of the baseball rule book.

Throughout the summer the Tigers battled for the division lead in a tight four-way race. Baseball analysts predicted that Detroit would wilt in the late summer sun because so many of their starting players were over thirty. As the division race continued late into the season, the Tigers did not wilt. Woodie Fryman, a thirty-two-year-old pitcher picked up by Martin in early August after being cast off by the Philadelphia Phillies, won ten straight games. Eddie Brinkman, thirty, set a record at shortstop by committing only seven errors all season. Al Kaline, thirty-seven, came back after pulling a hamstring muscle, which had sidelined him for a month, and hit .500 in the final weeks of the season. First baseman Norm Cash, thirty-seven, wound up with 22 home runs.

Martin alternately bullied and praised his players, driving them by any method he thought would be effective. He antagonized outfielder Jim Northrup—according to teammate Mickey Stanley, this made Northrup that much more determined to play his best. Martin spent time trying to cajole the best out of Willie Horton, whose reputation as a moody hypochondriac was as great as his reputation as a power hitter.

The division championship had not been decided as the Tigers went into the final series of the season at Boston— the Red Sox were neck and neck with Detroit. Mickey Lolich, thirty-two, struck out 15 Red Sox in the first game, and Kaline hit a home run as the Tigers won, 4–1. The next night, Woodie Fryman held Boston to one run, Kaline stroked the winning hit, and Detroit clinched the championship. In his third year of managing, Billy Martin had won his second championship. Smiling and wet-eyed, he sat in the clubhouse after the game, swigging from a bottle of champagne. "The players decide if we win or lose," he said, with unaccustomed modesty.

The 1972 playoff with the Oakland A's was among the most dramatic baseball series ever played. Oakland was favored. They had won their division for the second straight year, and had speed, power, pitching, and youth. In the first game, at Oakland, the score was tied 1–1 at the end of nine. After two more scoreless innings, Al Kaline stepped to the plate in the top of the eleventh and hit a home run, to give Detroit a one-run lead. In the bottom of the eleventh Oakland scored twice, on two singles and then a throwing error by Kaline, to win 3–2. John "Blue Moon" Odom threw a three-hitter at Detroit in the second game, and the A's won easily, 5–0. Only one game away from defeat, Martin still demanded victory from his players. He would not let them quit, and they did not quit. In the third game, in Detroit, Bill Freehan hit a homer and a double, and pitcher Joe Coleman shut out the A's, for a 3–0 victory. The fourth game was a pitching duel between Mickey Lolich and Catfish Hunter, and once again the score was tied 1–1 at the end of nine. The A's then scored two runs in the top of the tenth. Again the Tigers came back, scoring three in the bottom of the inning to win the game. Detroit took a 1–0 lead in the first inning of the final game. The A's scored once in the second and once in the fourth, and this time Detroit could not come up with a late rally. They lost the pennant in a 2–1 game.

Billy was unhappy, as he always was about losing. His frustration was greater this time, because he came within a run of the pennant, and he knew this might have been his last chance for a while. The Tigers were growing old and his farm system was not providing the young players he needed to replace the veterans.

Martin always felt that his relationship with Tiger owner John E. Fetzer was a good one. However, General Manager Jim Campbell and Billy Martin were no longer on the best of terms by the time spring training for the 1973 season opened in Lakeland, Florida. Martin thought he was being subjected to front-office interference, and his never-very-long temper shortened. Liable to boil over at any time, for any reason, he exploded at a young minor-leaguer, Ike Blessitt, outside a Lakeland bar early one morning and the incident wound up in the papers.

Late in spring training, Martin benched Willie Horton. By this time Campbell had been talking directly with many of the players. And he objected to the way Martin handled the star slugger. Billy announced he was quitting as manager of the Tigers, and walked out of the camp. One day later, he was talked into returning. "Campbell promised me that no player would go to him without going through me," Billy said later. But the practice continued.

Willie Horton continued to be a bone of contention between Campbell and Martin during the 1973 season. Looking back at the controversy four years later, though, Horton had only praise for his ex-manager. "I can thank Billy Martin that I'm playing this season," he said. Horton credited the self-discipline Martin taught him for his success in coming back from an injury. "Everything got exaggerated when we were together at Detroit. I never had an argument with the man, and I know he likes me. I'm just afraid that somewhere along the way he got the idea I didn't like him. Maybe there were misunderstandings. But he motivates a club. I'm a better ballplayer because of him. He made me sit on the bench for a year, and in that year I learned more about being a baseball player than in all the seasons I played."

Detroit did not look like a championship team in the early weeks of the season. Shortstop Eddie Brinkman started making errors. Mickey Lolich won only two of his first seven decisions. Al Kaline injured a groin muscle and had to be sidelined. In mid-May the little-regarded Milwaukee Brewers were in first place. Billy Martin was chagrined and he did not mind saying so. "It would be embarrassing if Milwaukee won the pennant," he told a Milwaukee reporter." I mean, how would it look to have a bunch of guys who are only making thirteen thousand dollars taking home twenty-two thousand in World Series shares?" Martin even complained about the Milwaukee organist's playing. He was kidding the Milwaukee reporter, but his kidding had an edge of frustration to it. On Detroit's next visit to Milwaukee, 41,000 fans came out to boo Martin, proving once again Martin's unique ability among managers to boost attendance. The girl who swept the bases between innings swatted the Detroit manager on his butt with her broom, to Billy's amusement as well as the crowd's.

Martin displayed little amusement in '73 over what he saw as the continued failure to enforce laws of baseball against Gaylord Perry. Managers are not supposed to criticize league presidents and baseball commissioners publicly, and few ever have. Early in the season, though, Martin began tearing into the president and the commissioner, saying what many managers often said in private. "Gutless" was the word Martin most often used. Campbell did not like that kind of outspokenness, and he told Billy to quiet down. Martin did not like to be told what not to say.

Campbell had grown tired of the manager's excesses, and watched his conduct closely. Responding to their tense manager's demands, the Tigers struggled to first place. Then, in August, the team went on a Western road trip with disastrous results—they fell out of first down to third, six games out. Campbell noted that Martin skipped a charter flight from Oakland to Chicago to check on some business interests in Kansas City. Campbell found out that Martin did not show up for the Chicago game until forty minutes before game time. After the Tigers dropped a doubleheader to the White Sox, eliminating Detroit from serious contention, Martin publicly blasted the Tiger farm bosses, Eddie Katalinas and Hoot Evers, for failing to provide him with the young players he needed in order to win. Campbell did not like Martin's behavior at all.

At the end of August, umpires rejected Martin's accusation that Gaylord Perry was again throwing illegal pitches in a shutout game against the Tigers. Martin then announced that he had ordered his pitchers, Joe Coleman and Fred Scherman, to use spitballs in the game as a protest. American League president Joe Cronin immediately suspended Martin for three days. The fact was Martin had not ordered the spitters. Coleman and Scherman admitted later they had decided on their own to doctor the ball. "All Billy was doing was sticking up for his players," Coleman said.

On the third day of Martin's suspension Jim Campbell fired his manager. Martin had one year remaining on his two-year contract. Campbell said the suspension was a "contributing factor" but that the firing resulted from an "accumulation of things." "There comes a point where what's right is right and what's wrong is wrong," the general manager explained. "From foul line to foul line Billy had done a good job. But there were a lot of other circumstances. There was a breakdown in company-policy matters. I had cautioned Billy about making public remarks about the commissioner, the American League president, Tiger executives, and our minor-league players. You just can't have that sort of thing. It breaks down the efficiency of your whole organization.

"I kicked around all the different angles," he said. "I weighed the pros and cons, and I made my decision. Once I had made up my mind, I advised Mr. Fetzer and he agreed with me. But it was my decision and I'll take full resonsibility for it."

The Detroit players, for the most part, were silent. "I can't say I was surprised," Norm Cash said, "but I don't want to elaborate."

"I never thought it would happen, knowing he had one year remaining on his contract," said Al Kaline. "He had some problems with a couple of players. But the last couple of weeks were very hectic."

Martin was angry. "Did I or did I not do a job for them?" he demanded. "When they needed me, I came in and did the job. This team was at its lowest ebb, after all that business with McLain. The powers that be felt they needed me then. And didn't I give them a winner? My record speaks for itself. I'll live and die with what I've done here. I'm going to bow out gracefully. I'll let Jim Campbell explain to the whole world why he fired me. If I had it to do all over again, I wouldn't do anything differently.

"Apparently winning and drawing people to the park aren't enough," Martin added. "I've done it twice and been fired both times."

Third-base coach Joe Schultz, hired by Martin, was

named as interim manager until the end of the season. "The team was always so tense," Schultz said after Martin was axed, "because we weren't sure what Billy was going to do next, personally or strategically."

The Tigers relaxed with Billy gone. They finished the 1973 season in third place. In 1974 and 1975 they relaxed all the way to last place in the Eastern Division. Martin continued his intense style of managing elsewhere.

Chapter 13
DISSENSION

Tensions exist on all teams—whether they're pennant winners or cellar dwellers. But a Billy Martin team, even when it's winning, plays under greater stress than most. Martin's driving need to win every game and his personal unpredictability create an emotionally charged atmosphere.

"It's hard to know what to do for him," one Yankee said. "He drives us hard. Guys who drive themselves hard, like Nettles and Munson, don't complain. But some guys do bitch. He's gotten on my ass, chewed me out when I didn't even think I'd done anything wrong. Billy likes guys who play like he did. He'd prefer everyone to be fiery."

Some Yankees, the fiery, openly aggressive ones, felt they had good communications with their manager. Some felt ill at ease around him. Martin spent little time in idle chatter with them. His intensity made them shy away from attempts at personal contact.

With these strains, plus the usual belief all players have that they deserve more playing time, some blowups between Billy and his '76 Yankees were inevitable. Martin knew this. The Doyle Alexander explosion did not surprise him. One of his managing maxims has always been: "Keep the five guys who hate you away from the five who are undecided." However well he kept them from one another, he could not always keep them away from the press.

On August 22 the Yankees came to bat in the bottom of the ninth, eight runs behind the California Angels. Yankee batters had only managed two hits and no runs for eight innings. Martin knew his team had lost. His only hope now was to avoid the disgrace of a shutout. Then, unexpectedly, the Yankee bats exploded like a rebirth of the Murderers' Row, scoring eight runs to send the game into extra innings. Billy and the entire team came alive, shouting their excitement at the most dramatic last-inning comeback they'd ever participated in.

In the top of the tenth, relief pitcher Sparky Lyle came to the mound. Though he had not been very effective in his last two appearances, he had been a major contributor to New York's success all season. It was his fifty-seventh relief stint in 120 Yankee games. With the score tied, if the Yankees eventually won, he would be credited with the win, his eighth. And after that dramatic ninth inning, a Yankee victory seemed inevitable. Lyle held the Angels scoreless in the tenth. In the eleventh he gave up a single to the leadoff batter. The next Angel bunted. Lyle fielded the ball, but his throw to second was too leisurely to catch the runner. It was the kind of play Martin hated. "I couldn't get planted to throw," Lyle said later. After a strikeout, Tommy Davis singled and the runner on second headed home. The throw from left hit the runner and ricocheted toward the Yankee dugout, where Lyle, backing up the play, fielded it. Sparky hesitated before throwing to the catcher—too late. A third runner scored before the inning was over. The Yankees scored none in the bottom of the eleventh and lost the game, wasting their astonishing comeback.

After the game Martin dressed quickly and marched out of the clubhouse without a word to anyone. Lyle sat at his locker, blaming himself. "We lost because I was horseshit," he said.

Billy Martin said little to Sparky over the next few weeks. When he needed a relief pitcher, he called on Dick Tidrow or Grant Jackson. Lyle came in from the bullpen only once in the next eighteen games. He resented not being used, but he said nothing to his manager.

After a Yankee win over the Red Sox on September 7, Martin was asked why he had not been using Sparky. Billy said that it was just because his other relief pitchers were so hot. A reporter asked if Lyle had to prove himself to Martin again in order to be used. "I'm a Sparky Lyle man," Billy answered. "He don't have to show me anything. I haven't used him, but he's been straight-out super about it. He went through a rough streak, but I still have all the confidence in the world in him. I was going to bring him in tonight after Tidrow if Tidrow got in trouble." Asked if he had spoken with Lyle about all this, Martin said he had, "in a roundabout way." Some of the reporters in Martin's office headed for the door. "Hey," Billy called after them. "Now you're going to go to Sparky and tell him what I said. Come back and tell me what he says."

The reporters gathered around Sparky's locker and told him what his manager had said. Did he want to comment? He did. "Roundabout?" he said. "What's that? By carrier pigeon? I don't care if he ever talks to me. I don't care if any manager ever talks to me. But then they run you into a game and wonder why the hell you don't pitch well. The longer I stay out, the more fouled up I get. I'm the one guy who can't sit time after time and have good stuff. Any dumb SOB knows that."

He was asked if the "dumb SOB" theory included his manager. "Including him," Lyle said.

"Whatever he says to you," Sparky continued, speaking quietly, deliberately, with controlled anger, "you can count on it being the exact opposite. You can ask anybody. I've heard more instances of guys' hating him. I liked him until I saw some of the stuff that was going on. He said to me on the plane going to California, 'Have you had enough rest?' I said, 'Yeah, more than enough.' Then he said, 'I'm going to start using you.' I said to myself right then and there that meant he probably wouldn't pitch me. I would've felt a lot better if he had come up to me and said, 'You're throwing lousy. We're trying to win this thing and until you show you're out of it, I'm only going to use you in games we're losing, because the other guys are going well.' That's better than beating around the bush and saying, 'Well, I'm planning on using you.'"

The word was brought from Sparky's locker back to Martin's office. Billy did not like the public communications, but he kept cool. "Sparky wants to pitch," he said. "I can understand that. I don't ever panic, over him or anybody. But you have to keep the ballclub in consideration. A guy gets jocked five times in a row and the club gets down. Sometimes when you do what you think is right you hurt somebody. But if you're a manager, that's part of the job.

"Sparky is going to get a lot of pitching in before the end of the season," Martin continued. "Just as soon as I get the opportunity, I'm going to use him two, three innings so he can get sharp."

In the next three games no relief pitchers were necessary. Then Martin called on Sparky for relief in the eighth inning of a close game with Detroit. Lyle finished the game allowing no runs, though the Yankees lost. That week Martin and Lyle had "a nice little talk," as Martin called it. "What happened was really nothing," Martin explained to reporters. "He was frustrated and he thought [pitching coach] Bob Lemon or I should have talked to him about it. So he let his frustrations hang out in the press. Now he's my main left-hander out of the bullpen the next four days. I want him sharp for the playoffs."

Three days later, with the Yankees protecting an 8–1

lead late in the game and Grant Jackson tiring, Martin called for Lyle in the bullpen. "Billy asked me if I wanted to pitch," a grim-faced Lyle said later, "and I said no." Lyle refused to elaborate. "I wanted to pitch both Lyle and Tidrow one inning apiece," Martin explained, "but Lyle said he didn't want to throw tonight. Sometimes that's the way pitchers are. That's all right. He's done that before. I called down and asked if he wants to pitch in a game that's not close—I always give him the option."

On September 12, before a Sunday doubleheader with Detroit, Martin talked about the problems of his job. "It's tough being a manager," he said. "Coaching was a breeze. It was fun. No pressure. But sitting in this chair . . .

"I like all the guys. I like Sparky; I really do. But he's mad at me now," Martin said, with no rancor in his voice. "I'd sure like to have Casey around now, to ask him how he handled it, not using a guy. I wish he'd lived ten more years."

As Martin talked in his office, less than two hours before the game, players were still drifting into the clubhouse. The team rules, posted on the clubhouse door, said that all players had to show up two hours before game time. Martin rarely worried about players' coming in later as long as they showed up for batting practice, or, if batting practice was optional that day, at least well before the game began. Game time today was one o'clock. At twelve-thirty Martin noticed that Mickey Rivers was missing. Billy made out two lineup cards—one with Rivers on it, one without. He waited in his office until just before one. Then he handed the lineups to Dick Howser, telling him to give the umpire the one with Rivers on it if he showed up in time. Mickey did not arrive until Howser had already handed in the lineup card.

After the doubleheader, reporters surrounded Rivers to ask why he was not in the lineup for the first game. Mickey, speaking in a depressed monotone, said he had been stuck in traffic. Martin had been angry, he admitted, when he arrived only minutes before the game. What did Billy say? "What any manager would say," Mickey responded. He also confessed he had been fined but would not say for how much.

Rivers, knowing he was at fault, did not push his traffic excuse too hard. But he had something else on his mind, and as long as he was surrounded by newsmen asking questions, he decided to bring it out. "There's a lack of communication between us," Mickey said. "Last week, in Baltimore, I took my wife on the road trip. He said that anybody bringing their wife on the road would be fined. I like taking my wife on the road. I didn't know there was no rule you can't bring your wife along—ain't no rule like that. Other wives have been on trips. Why'd he say it? I don't know. That's why I say there's a lack of communications. Since then we've been this far apart," Rivers said, stretching his hands out.

Martin was not happy to hear the news that Rivers was complaining. His feet on his desk, his eyes on the football game on his portable TV, Martin sipped from a can of beer while he answered questions about Rivers' lateness.

"When he got here, the cards had already been handed to the umpire. He's lucky I didn't really chew his ass out," Martin said. "That's a no-no, pal. He made a mistake today. If he didn't say anything about it, I wouldn't have."

When a reporter asked Martin about the no-wives-on-the-road rule, he avoided answering. "That's another subject," he said. The reporters made it clear they already had Mickey's version. Martin's mouth tightened. "From now on the wives are going to have to get permission from me to go on a road trip. I don't want wives sneaking into different towns," Martin said. "I know what it does to players. Players worry about their wives getting to and from the ballpark. But all they have to do is check through me for my permission, and ninety-nine times out of a hundred they'll get it.

"I did that to make an effect on Mickey," he explained. "It

didn't have to do with his wife. But Mickey went to the trainer's room the night after his wife got there and said he couldn't play. His wife comes to town and he says his legs are bothering him. It's not like a honeymoon on the road when you're fighting for a pennant."

Yogi Berra interrupted the interview, sticking his head into Billy's office to tell him goodnight. He was dressed nattily and Martin asked him where he was going. "To a wedding," Berra said. "See if you can talk the guy out of it," Billy called after him.

Mickey Rivers' expression changed from moody depression to anger when he was told what Martin had said about his wife's joining him on the road. Mickey had started in the first three games after his wife arrived in Baltimore, then played the last innings of the fourth. "I didn't say I couldn't play," he snapped. "If he said that, he's lying,"

After the newspaper articles appeared the next day, communications between the star center fielder and the manager did not improve. As much as Billy Martin enjoys a good fight, he does not like fights within a team—and he does not like internal dissension being exposed to the public. "It's frustrating," Martin said, later in the year. "You get to feel for the players like they're your own children; then you read a player's comments about you. Talk to them face to face and it's different."

One man observed the late-season blowups around him with sardonic amusement. Elliott Maddox, a bright, independent-minded black player, had his blowup with Martin before Billy became Yankee manager. Maddox spent most of the summer of '76 on the disabled list, his surgically repaired knee still bothering him. On September 1 he was returned to the roster. Martin, who has said he would play Hitler if he were the best man for the position, platooned Maddox against left-handers in September games, as rightfielder or designated hitter. Relations between the two remained distant.

Asked if Elliott was happy playing, Martin answered coolly, "I don't know. I haven't asked him. I'm happy. The players like him, so they're happy."

Elliott's knee pained him every time he moved it, to the point that he decided to have a postseason operation without the Yankee doctor's permission, paying for it himself. And yet, he was happy to be playing. Asked in the clubhouse after a game if he had anything to say about his manager, Elliott combed his hair, and after a long, pregnant pause, he said, "Nothing of interest." He flashed his good-humored smile, knowing he did not have to say anything more. He had not changed his opinion of Martin since playing for him in Texas.

In early September, 1973, less than a week after Detroit fired Billy Martin, Bob Short, principal owner of the Texas Rangers, fired his manager, Whitey Herzog. On September 8, Martin, wearing a new baseball uniform, was managing the Rangers. "I'd fire my grandmother if I had a chance to get Billy Martin," Short explained. He knew Martin well. Billy had helped him in his unsuccessful campaign for governor of Minnesota a few years earlier.

"I just wanted to forget baseball for a while," Martin said. "I was hurt by what had happened, and I wanted to get away from it all. Only because Bob asked me did I come down for the final month." Martin would have much preferred to take over as manager at the beginning of the next season, and give his tangled nerves a chance to sort themselves out. Short's offer was attractive—a three-year contract, with a salary exceeding his $65,000 from Detroit, plus incentive payments and living expenses. Besides, Martin looked forward to working with Bob Short. Here, Billy felt, was one man who understood him, one man with whom he could have a smooth working relationship. "I have to manage my way. Sometimes I step on some toes, but here I think there's less chance because communication is sound," Martin said. "I like to work with someone who knows Billy Martin, and Bob Short knows me."

It was too late in the season to make any drastic changes on the Rangers. They won 9 of their 23 games under Martin in the final month and finished with a 57–105 record, the worst in the majors. Billy liked the challenge. He claimed to see winning potential in the team's youth and speed. After the season, instead of talking about rebuilding programs or respectability for the coming season, he talked about winning.

Martin said the Rangers would be contending for the championship in 1974. "I not only believe it, I'm staking my reputation on it," Billy proclaimed, "and my baseball reputation means a lot to me. I believe I can do it basically with the people who are here. Right now, people are laughing at us, I know that. And people also laugh when I say we'll be a contending team next season. But let's wait and see who's laughing next season."

"He was the biggest optimist since General Custer told his troops to take no prisoners," Martin's new third-base coach, Frank Lucchesi, later commented.

"Losing is just like winning. It becomes a habit," Martin said before spring training. "These guys are tired of losing. In spring training we are going to show them how to win. When they see our program, they are going to believe they can win."

In spring training the players began to believe their manager. Martin also made some changes. Mike Hargrove, a twenty-four-year-old who had never played higher than Class-A ball, caught Billy's eye. Martin kept him on the squad, and Hargrove wound up as Rookie of the Year. When the Chicago Cubs decided to dump fading pitcher Ferguson Jenkins, Martin picked him up. Jenkins went on to a 25–12 record, winning the Comeback-of-the-Year award. Martin also decided that part-time outfielder Elliott

Maddox could not hit major-league pitching, so the Rangers sold Maddox to the Yankees. Elliott already had bitter feelings for Martin. Maddox had played for Detroit in 1970, and he blamed Martin, who had been named Tiger manager at the end of that season, for shipping him to Washington, the Rangers' predecessor team, in October, 1970. Now he said Martin had promised him a shot at playing regularly with the Rangers and had not lived up to his promise.

The 1974 Rangers did not resemble the Ranger teams of the past—they won games. And Martin drove them, hard. He had promised a winner and his reputation was on the line. "I remember one time some pitcher forgot to cover first base," infielder Jim Fregosi said. "The next day he had the whole staff out there covering first base for half an hour or more. Billy never said a word. I don't think anybody messed up on that the rest of the season." Martin also kept players on their toes by being unpredictable. "You can't figure him out. Billy's liable to do anything at any time," Fregosi said.

Outfielder Jeff Burroughs described Martin's effect on the club. "He hates to lose," he said, "and when he does, he lets you know about it. He really gets upset when you do dumb mental things. After a game that you lose, he's angry, and you figure if he's going to act like that, let's bust our butts a little more and win. It's all psychological and it's the believability of the manager. Some managers don't mean it. Billy does."

The Rangers soon demonstrated in the usual way that they had become a Billy Martin team—with a spirited brawl on the field. In an early June game with Cleveland in Texas, brushback pitches were exchanged until Martin's troops ran on the field to battle the enemy. The manager himself was in the thick of his players and it was reported later than Martin was knocked down twice during the melee. "I was not," Billy objected. "I was *pushed* down twice. There's a difference, you know."

The following week, the Rangers played in Cleveland, on

Ten Cent Beer Night. In the seventh inning the Ranger bullpen had to move into the dugout to escape barrages of firecrackers, smoke bombs and empty beer cups from the Indian fans. In the ninth inning, with the score tied 5–5, some fans jumped out of the stands to attack right fielder Jeff Burroughs. As the other Rangers ran from their positions, the rest of the team charged from the dugout to come to their comrade's aid. By this time members of the crowd were pouring out of the stands, many of them wielding chairs. The Cleveland dugout also emptied as the team rushed to help their fellow ballplayers. When it became clear that the situation was too dangerous to resume the game, Cleveland forfeited.

Afterward Martin smiled with pride. "Jeff was out there all by himself," he said. "I saw knives and chairs and other things. We just couldn't let our teammate get beat up.

"I'm very proud of the Cleveland players," he added, generously. "They saved our lives."

While the Rangers were transforming from losers to winners on the field, their front office also did some changing. Bob Short sold his controlling shares, a new ownership and management group took over, and Martin began to clash with them. He told General Manager Dan O'Brien that David Clyde, the local fireballing teenager, should be sent down to the minors. In baseball terms Martin was clearly right, but Clyde had been one of the Rangers' few gate attractions. People had been paying to see him pitch. When Martin was told no, he threatened to quit. The answer was still no. Billy thought more about it, and decided not to quit.

When Martin did show his temper, his target was the team's publicist and traveling secretary, Burt Hawkins, a former sportswriter in his late fifties. Hawkins's wife had been asked by the wife of the new club president, Bobby Brown, to help her form a Rangers' wives' club. When Martin got wind of the idea, he vetoed it. Billy does not believe wives should have any role in the exclusive men's club of baseball. They only threatened morale.

On a late-season charter flight, after a doubleheader defeat, the subject of the wives' club came up again. Martin said Hawkins's wife had started the whole idea. Hawkins denied it, and the two argued. Then Martin slapped Hawkins. When the incident became public, Billy apologized. President Bobby Brown announced he had placed Billy Martin on "probation," which really meant no action had been taken.

The incident was quickly forgotten in Texas, in the excitement of the team's first successful year. The Rangers finished in second place with an 84–76 record, five games behind the division-winning Oakland A's. Individually, the Rangers played over their heads. Jeff Burroughs was a good player, but not quite as good as his 25 home runs, 118 RBIs, .301 average and Most Valuable Player award indicated. Mike Hargrove, who jumped from Class-A ball and won Rookie of the Year, batted .323 because his manager convinced him he could do it. Once again, Billy Martin had proved himself a winner, perhaps even a baseball genius. He had turned teams into winners before, but never so dramatically. He had staked his reputation on a promise to make the worst team in the majors into a contender, and he had done it. Martin was named Manager of the Year by the Associated Press. (*The Sporting News* picked Yankee manager Bill Virdon.)

Martin looked forward to the 1975 season with confidence. He predicted the Rangers would win the American League pennant this time. "A lot of people laughed last year, too," he said, with pride. "The little Dago must know what he's doing."

Billy felt secure in his job. "I have a real foundation here," he said. "I think I'll stay here the rest of my career." He lived near the Rangers' park, in Arlington, in a house the Rangers had provided for him. His ten-year-old son,

Billy Joe, was enrolled in the parochial school there and enjoyed his new home. "I try to include Billy Joe in everything I can when I'm home," Martin said. "We have some wonderful times. Oh, it's so exciting, that kind of love."

Billy's friend Mickey Mantle lived nearby, in Dallas, where he was a vice-president of Reserve Life Insurance. "I was the happiest man in the world when Billy got the job down here," Mickey said, "because it gave me somebody to hang around with."

Though he had some front-office conflicts in 1974, Billy's relationship with majority stockholder Brad Corbett, a plastic-pipe and chemical executive ten years his junior, had been smooth so far, and Martin did not expect any serious trouble. By spring training, the only cloud Martin could see on the horizon—no bigger than an outfielder's glove, but growing—was Elliott Maddox. After being sold to the Yankees, Maddox had become a star. As Yankee centerfielder, he performed as an outstanding defensive player, hit .303, and finished in the top ten in MVP balloting. People would point to him as proof that Martin, for all his success, could make major mistakes in assessing talent. Worse, Maddox had sounded off to the newspapers, calling Martin a "liar" for promising him a shot at a starting position and then dumping him. That was a personal challenge and Elliott would have to answer for it.

"I don't dislike Elliott Maddox at all," Martin claimed. "He hates me because I never played him. I never liked his makeup, his laziness, his show-offishness. When I sold him to New York, I was doing him a favor, keeping him in the big leagues. Then he has one good year and becomes a big mouth."

In the first spring training game of 1975 between the Rangers and the Yankees, Maddox stepped up to bat against pitcher Jim Bibby. A fastball hit him on the shoulder. Later another Ranger pitcher, Stan Thomas, threw a pitch that skimmed over Maddox's head. Yankee pitcher

Mike Wallace retaliated for his team, throwing two pitches that narrowly missed the head of Dave Nelson, and soon both teams were on the field, scuffling.

After the game, several Yankees had acid comments to make about Martin. "How would it look," asked pitcher Rudy May, "if I knocked down a Texas player just because he said something about Virdon? Let them settle it with each other." Mike Wallace added, "If Nelson wants to get hot at somebody, he should get hot at his manager for being put in that position. It's childish. I think Martin has an ego problem. It's a ridiculous position to put his players in. He's not the one who's going to get beaned—they are."

Martin proclaimed his innocence. "He might have been thrown at," Billy said, "but not under orders from me. They brushed him off because they know Elliott Maddox gets scared to death when someone comes close enough. My players were madder than I was. They know I value honesty, and I'd been fair with Maddox even though I thought he was lazy and arrogant. So they brushed him back without my orders."

Martin's feud with Maddox was not over. Early in the regular season, Stan Thomas again threw at Maddox, hitting him on the elbow and forcing him out of the game. The next inning Ranger catcher Jim Sundberg was scheduled to lead off. Everyone knew a retaliation pitch was coming. Martin pulled Sundberg back and sent up little-used reserve catcher Bill Fahey to pinch hit, or pinch-be-hit, in this case. Fahey ducked one high-and-tight pitch and another behind-the-head pitch by Catfish Hunter. After the game, in which three batters were hit, Martin said he was "surprised and shocked" Fahey was thrown at. "But I couldn't fault Hunter. He's got to protect his own players," Martin said. "The Maddox pitch wasn't even up and in on him. I think he wants to get hit so he can cry. Maddox is a big baby. What he needs is a good ass-kicking."

"You're just the one to do it," a bystander suggested.

"That would be so easy it'd be ridiculous," Martin said.

Billy had promised the pennant this year. When the Rangers lagged, Martin's temper grew short, especially with umpires. In one game he charged out to argue that rookie umpire Richard Garcia had called a ground ball fair only after checking with third-base umpire Ron Luciano. Luciano was Martin's least-favorite umpire, and Billy swore that he had seen Luciano give a fair-ball signal. When Martin's arguing became vehement, Garcia threw him out of the game.

In the clubhouse later, Martin puffed on his pipe and commented to several reporters, "Truth—I don't think you see much of it anymore."

"They're out to get me," he added. "Two National League umpires asked me in spring training why the umpires in my league were all out to get me. And if they're out to get me, it will be very difficult for my ballclub to win this year. I've got to protect myself and my team."

Billy came up with a scheme of defense against the umpires. He ordered his pitching coach, Art Fowler, to find him a microphone and a tape recorder. During the next day's game, Martin wore the mike clipped to his uniform. Although it was not plugged in, the microphone was in Luciano's full view every time Martin approached him for an exchange of opinion. The gesture seemed to imply that the Ranger manager was ready to ship tapes to the league office if Luciano said anything incriminating. "I want to get him fired," Martin explained.

"He wants to win, I think, more than any other human being in the world," was Luciano's comment on Martin's conduct. "Texas is a very physical team," he added. "They go into second very hard. They're a big, strong, scrappy team—rah, rah, boom-boom, college go-go-go. That's from Martin all the way."

The college try was not working as well this season as it had in '74. The players who totally trusted their manager last season were more skeptical now. He said the team would win the pennant, but first place was growing ever more distant as the season progressed. Maybe, they thought, Billy Martin could be wrong. The more the Rangers lost, the more tense and difficult the manager became.

"He began to second-guess us unmercifully," one Ranger remembered later. "Since nothing is ever Billy's fault, everything had to be blamed on somebody. It got where he seemed to think we wanted to screw up, just to get at him."

Some of the Rangers had already been disaffected by the Maddox incidents. "His tough-guy image became a joke then," said one bitter player later. "We thought, if he hated Elliott so much, why didn't he wait for him after a game and beat him up? Instead he used his pitchers to hurt a guy."

As the team continued to fall behind Oakland, Billy's relationship with the press also became more strained than usual. During one road trip he yelled at a writer, "Why do you have to write negative things? Don't you care if we win?"

Martin's final confrontation, inevitably, came with the front office. Brad Corbett, the majority stockholder, had been defending his manager against the negative opinions of most of the other stockholders, until he took a trip with the team before the All-Star game. "Several players came up to me and expressed their views about the situation," he said later. "I was shocked. So I conducted my own survey. I met with nearly every player on the team privately and asked for their views. The overwhelming opinion was that this team was in trouble.

"The young players are the heart of this team," Corbett continued. "Frankly, there was a division between these young players and Billy that was most detrimental to this team."

Still, Corbett hesitated about making a move. Then Martin forced the issue. Billy wanted to pick up the contract of a journeyman catcher, Tom Egan, who had been released by the Angels. General Manager Dan O'Brien was against the move. At a meeting on Saturday, July 19, Corbett sided with O'Brien, seeing the acquisition out of keeping with the youth movement Corbett favored. "We've got enough of those kind of veterans around here already," he said. Billy lost his temper and shouted at the owner. He pulled off the $500 wristwatch Corbett had given him for Christmas and smashed it against the wall of his office. Corbett left the office in a rage. That Monday, July 21, with the fourth-place Rangers sporting a 44–51 record and trailing 15½ games behind Oakland, Martin told his morning-radio-show audience that he expected to be fired.

Late that afternoon Billy cleaned out his locker. "It had become like a country club down here," he complained. "I couldn't keep control of my players. People want a 'yes man,' somebody who says 'yessir.' Well, you can't win doing it that way." As he stuffed clothes into a duffel bag, he spoke about Corbett. "He knows as much about baseball as I know about pipe. One year in baseball and he's a genius."

Reporters immediately relayed Martin's comments to Corbett, who was in his Arlington Stadium office, working on the official announcement of Martin's firing. He came right down to the clubhouse and had a closed-door meeting with Martin. When the two came out, Martin told waiting newsmen, "I said some things earlier that I now regret."

Asked what he had said to Martin, Corbett replied, "I just asked him if he was being fair to himself, being fair to me and being fair to this ballclub when he made those kinds of statements."

In his statement later, at a press conference before the night game, Corbett said, "I recognize this will cause a trauma with the fans. . . . The fan reaction will be tough. As a student of the game, Billy was one of the finest, but there are causes for his firing beyond his won-lost record."

Before the start of the game, Billy stood in the clubhouse

and wept as he shook hands with various team members and the press. Asked about his future, he said, "I don't know. I love this game. Baseball is my life. But at this very moment I feel like telling the game to shove it. I don't think I can come back into baseball. Of course, I'm saying that right now, without any sleep in two days. I think a manager must live and manage by his convictions, so he gets fired by his convictions. I've had plenty of experience in both. But I want to go on record that there are no hard feelings, no recriminations. I'm not throwing any rocks at anyone.

"I'm happy about one thing," Martin concluded. "I brought Texas a winner. I brought them a million fans, and I brought them some real major-league baseball."

Most of the players would say only "no comment" about the firing. Later one of them told Pete Axthelm of *Newsweek*, "Have you noticed that whenever Billy gets fired, the fans and press scream but the players are remarkably quiet?"

Within ten days, Billy Martin was the manager of the New York Yankees. In a little more than a year, he was manager of the American League pennant winner and, again, AP's Manager of the Year.

Texas finished the 1975 season in third place. In 1976 they dropped to fifth.

Chapter 14
RETURN TO GLORY

On Saturday night, September 25, 1976, echoes of the past reverberated throughout New York City's gathering places—quietly in expensive midtown restaurants, noisily in neighborhood bars. That afternoon the Yankees had clinched the Eastern Division championship. They hadn't won the pennant yet, but they had won something. And New Yorkers felt like their old selves of a dozen years ago, when New York was great and the Yankees were its proud symbol.

Since the last Yankee pennant, in 1964, the New York Mets had won two pennants and one World Series. The Met triumphs, however, were unlike those of the old Yankees. Met victories were ironic, unexpected, the occasional success of a born loser. The Mets represented New York's self-deprecating view of itself; the Yankees, its arrogance. Now, New Yorkers could once again believe in the Yankees, and a little more in themselves. For the American League championship series against the Kansas City Royals, the Yankees were favored, the way Yankees always were in the big stakes games. The experts *predicted* they would win; New Yorkers *knew* they would. And the players themselves were totally confident. They talked "three-game sweep."

For manager Billy Martin the echoes of the old Yankee glory rang across two decades, from the last time he had played on a Yankee championship team. He had forged that link between the Golden Age and today, and he was confident of its strength. He could imagine Casey Stengel telling him he had done well.

For Billy there were other, less pleasant memories in these playoffs. Kansas City itself was the site of his two most bitter moments as a Yankee. It was where he had been sent down to the minors in his rookie year, triggering his blowup at General Manager George Weiss; and where he had been traded when Weiss finally found an excuse to exile him. The current Kansas City baseball team, the Royals, were managed by Whitey Herzog, a good friend of Billy's. Herzog had been fired by the Texas Rangers to make room for Martin, two years before Billy was himself fired by the Rangers. Now the two ex-Ranger managers faced each other in the playoffs.

Martin had managed playoff teams twice before. Both times his teams had been underdogs, and both times they had lost. These playoffs, with Martin's first league pennant as the prize, were a personal test he could not fail again. He knew he would win—he had to win. For once his team was favored. If he lost, his critics would point to this as proof that Martin was not the winning manager he claimed to be.

Martin made the final cuts to select the Yankees' twenty-five-man roster for the playoffs and, he expected, the World Series. He made his selections based on ability, not on how well he liked a player; this was confirmed when he announced that he had retained Elliott Maddox and dropped Gene Locklear, a pinch hitter. Since Maddox's return from the disabled list at the beginning of September, Elliott had shown little at bat or in the field. He wore a massive knee brace and the knee obviously still bothered him. Martin could have easily defended replacing him with Locklear.

"I cut an American Indian to make room on my roster for a black man," said Martin, who was known to be partial to the cause of American Indians. "I picked Maddox over Locklear because I feel Ellie can contribute more in the playoffs. Locklear swings a good bat, but I can use Maddox in the outfield. He gives me more moves."

Despite the bad feelings between him and Martin, Maddox was, after all, a Yankee. And Martin had a Royal player on whom to focus his personal animosity. Herzog had named ex-Ranger and ex-Yankee Larry Gura as his opening-game pitcher. Though Gura had only a 4–0 record since being traded by New York to Kansas City, on May 16, he had been the winning pitcher in the only two victories the Royals had in their last eleven games. Since his trade, Gura had sounded off to newspaper reporters about his ex-manager, Billy Martin, frequently calling him a liar. His complaints paralleled those of Elliot Maddox.

At Texas in 1974 Martin sent Gura down to the minors after allowing him only one inning of pitching in spring training. That summer, the Rangers traded him to the Yankees, and by 1975 Gura had become a starting pitcher. Larry claimed that in spring training of 1976 Martin promised him regular work, then failed to keep his promise. Five weeks into the season, with Gura not having pitched an inning, he was traded to Kansas City for reserve catcher Fran Healy.

Before the playoffs, Gura was asked if he felt animosity toward Martin. "I do and then I don't," he said. "Sometimes I feel almost sorry for him. The lies—he's been like that his whole career. Maybe he's not the type to manage."

"I got rid of him in Texas because he couldn't get the ball over the plate in spring training," Martin said. "I got rid of him in New York because he wasn't as good as the other four starters we were using. And if I had him here now, I'd get rid of him again. I never promised him anything. I remember a lot of twelve-hitters, three-two counts, and the bases loaded all the time. He's the kind of guy who's got you on the end of the bench every inning."

Asked about Gura's eagerness to face the Yankees, Martin replied, "I think it might make him a worse pitcher. Sometimes a guy gets too keyed up and starts walking everyone. He's going to try to prove something, but I don't think my players are too pleased at the way he's been popping off."

Martin's players expressed no concern about Gura's comments. They were pleased with the opening-game match-up of Catfish Hunter and Larry Gura. "We've got a four-million-dollar pitcher going against a guy who was traded for Fran Healy," commented Lou Piniella in Fran's presence. "How can we lose?"

On Wednesday, October 6, the day before the Yankees flew to Kansas City, Martin leaned back in his office chair and discussed his plans with reporters. "I'm cutting off the players' telephones in the hotel," he confided. "I told them it was to keep them away from crank calls. Actually, it's so their girlfriends can't call them, since their wives will be there. That's why I made the rule that they had to check with me before they could bring their wives on the road," he added, referring to the Mickey Rivers incident. "It was for their sake. Some of them are so dumb their wives could sneak into town and catch them in bed with a broad."

No one asked Martin why he had never given that explanation to Mickey, who, unlike many of his teammates, liked having his wife on the road.

The Yankee manager announced that his second-game pitcher would be Ed Figueroa. Martin refused to reveal his choice for the third game. It could be Ken Holtzman, Doyle Alexander, or Dock Ellis. Billy said he had told the one who would be pitching, but not the other two. "If we put in the papers that the pitcher has been told, won't the other two then know?" one logical reporter asked. Martin said it was all a matter of strategy.

The next afternoon, the Yankees held a practice session on the Kansas City Astroturf. Then Billy went off with Munson and Hunter for some catfishing at a local pond.

By the time the first game of the playoffs started on Saturday, another Royal had added his name to Martin's enemies list. In a newspaper interview, George Brett, third baseman and league batting champion, accused Martin of lying to his brother Ken, a pitcher who had been traded by the Yankees to the Chicago White Sox early in the season. "Either Martin is lying about it," George said, discussing the circumstances of the trade, "or my brother's lying, and my brother doesn't lie."

When Larry Gura took the mound, Billy Martin's voice could be heard; yelling insults from the dugout. George Brett threw wildly to first after fielding Mickey Rivers' leadoff grounder, and Martin led the Yankee bench in razzing him—"Your brother could play better at third." "Hit it to Brett—he chokes." Brett made another throwing error in the first inning, allowing the Yankees a 2–0 lead, and the Yankee bench-jockeying grew even louder. Catfish Hunter looked very strong on the mound, like his old self after a season made shaky by a sore arm. On Billy's only visit to the mound, the manager said to Catfish about the next batter, "He's a first-ball fastball hitter. What are you going to throw him?" "A fastball," Catfish replied. Billy nodded, accepting his pitcher's judgment over the scouts', and trotted back to the dugout.

Martin's most direct contribution to the Yankees' 4–1 victory came in the eighth inning, when Royal shortstop Fred Patek singled with two out. As pinch hitter Jamie Quirk came to bat, Martin signaled for a pitchout. Martin had guessed Patek would be running on the first pitch. He was, and Munson's throw to Fred Stanley nailed him.

After the game, both Gura and Brett complained about

the riding Martin had given them. "He called me everything in the book," Brett said. "If they had a tape recorder
on him, it would be one long bleep." "He was calling me
some names, typical low class," said Gura. "Nothing you
can print." Larry was approached in the Royals' clubhouse
by a league official who asked him to come to the press-
interview room. "Is Martin gone?" Gura asked. "It's not
that I don't want to face him, but I'd rather not go there if
he's still there."

In the Yankee locker room Martin defended his bench-
jockeying. "I got on Brett for his statement in the papers
about his brother," Billy said. "I did it man to man, on the
field. That's the old way. Not in the papers. If Brett wants
to fight me, I ain't looking for it, but I ain't backing away,
either. The whole bench was on him. Does he want to fight
the whole team?

"This is no goody-goody-two-shoes party," Martin added.
"This is no high-school game. This is for a major-league
pennant. We're out to beat them—any way we can."

Martin was restrained in his comments about Gura. "He
pitched very well," Billy said. Then he added in a private
aside, "I want them to pitch him against us again." While
Billy was talking, a policeman came into the manager's
office and said, "Mr. Martin, we got a threat and we just
want to let you know why we're here. They threatened to
blow up the stadium."

"They lose hard here, don't they," said Billy.

The next day, the Kansas City fans were hard on Martin.
Before the game a group behind the home-plate screen
yelled a steady stream of insults at the Yankee manager.
After a while Martin answered one loud fan. "I bet you
wouldn't say that if this screen wasn't here. Is that nose of
yours for real? Go on, take it off. It can't be real."

"Yeah," the fan yelled back, "it's real, and it's as big as
yours. I dare you to come up here. You guys are through!"
Martin walked away with a smile.

When Billy came out to the mound in the sixth inning to lift starting pitcher Ed Figueroa, a torrent of boos descended. Billy ignored them while he waited on the mound for relief pitcher Dick Tidrow. On his walk back to the dugout, Billy smiled to the fans, and blew kisses. He grinned with enjoyment even back in the dugout. Almost everything important Billy Martin ever did in his life he did in front of thousands. He has learned to enjoy playing to or against a crowd.

Along with reviving the old-fashioned practice of bench-jockeying during the playoffs, the Yankees added a modern dimension to the game, suggested by former football coach George Steinbrenner. In the second game, two Yankee scouts sat in the radio booth, where there is a very good view of the field, and used walkie-talkies to send instructions on positioning outfielders to coach Gene Michael in the Yankee dugout.

The walkie-talkies didn't do the Yankees much good in the game. They committed five errors, more than in any game during the season; allowed three stolen bases; had one baserunning error; and stranded eleven runners on base. They lost 7–3. And Billy left himself open for second guessing. When Herzog went to lefty pitcher Paul Splittorff, Martin allowed his lefty-hitting platoon—Oscar Gamble and Carlos May—to remain in the game instead of bringing in Lou Piniella and Elliott Maddox, his right-hand-hitting platoon. In six at-bats against the Kansas City left-handers, May and Gamble combined for only one single.

"My left-handed hitters can hit left-handed pitching," Martin said in his defense. "They were hitting the ball hard."

"If our left-handed hitters can hit left-handed pitchers, why don't they start against left-handed pitchers?" Elliott Maddox complained. "I'm just glad Gura wasn't knocked out before I got up yesterday. If he had been, I'd still be looking for my first at-bat."

Martin also defended his team, which had played very sloppy baseball. "I don't pay attention to errors," he claimed. "My players are human and are going to make errors."

George Brett, who had four hits in seven at-bats in the first two games, said he could not hear much bench-jockeying during the second game. "Billy had a sore throat," he said with a smile, "or he outgrew it. I think this whole thing got overblown in the papers. I have some extra incentive—I wouldn't call it revenge. All I know is, I'd be very happy for myself, my team, and my brother if we beat him.

"All that stuff about us fighting—I don't want to fight anyone," he continued. "He's the last one I'd want to get into a fight with."

Whitey Herzog was gracious in victory. He mentioned that several short fly balls went for hits by the Royals. "The bloopers did it for us. They fell in and we were able to run on them and play our game," he said.

The Tuesday-night crowd at Yankee Stadium came armed with firecrackers and rolls of toilet paper. It was championship ball at the Stadium again—but the crowd differed from those that used to watch the champion Yankees of the '50s. Back then, the fans were cool and arrogant—they expected victory. Or they were anti-Yankee fans rooting for some underdog trying to knock off the inevitable champs. The '76 crowd was livelier, more partisan, and much noisier. When Mayor Abe Beame's young grandson Andrew threw out the first ball, he was roundly booed, though he had never done anything to the city.

The first inning did not give the Yankee fans much to cheer about, as the Royals reached Dock Ellis for three runs. In the fourth Chris Chambliss cut the Kansas City lead to 3–2 with a two-run homer. In the fifth Fred Patek was called out stealing second. The crowd was puzzled to see both Herzog and Martin race from their dugouts to protest. While Herzog argued that Patek was safe, Martin's beef was that Patek should have been thrown out of the game for throwing down his batting helmet.

In the sixth inning Herzog used five pitchers in an attempt to shut off a Yankee rally—without success. After Roy White walked and Munson doubled him to third, Herzog removed his starting pitcher, left-handed Andy Hassler, and brought in right-handed Marty Pattin to face righty Lou Piniella. Martin, playing by the book, pinch hit lefty Carlos May for Piniella. May was given a walk to load the bases, and Pattin was removed for lefty Tom Hall to pitch to lefty Chris Chambliss. Chris hit into a force play at second, scoring White from third. Graig Nettles followed with a single that drove in Munson. Herzog then brought in Steve Mingori, a lefty, to face right-handed Elliott Maddox, because Herzog wanted to hold his ace right-handed relief pitcher, Mark Littell, in reserve. He shouldn't have. Maddox hit a double to score Chambliss. Herzog then brought in Littell to retire the side.

The Yankees held on to their 5–3 lead through the end of the game. Martin had one surprise left, though. He removed a tired Dock Ellis at the end of eight and brought Sparky Lyle out of the doghouse to pitch the ninth. After walking the first batter, Lyle put down the next three to end the game.

"I was very surprised when I got the call," Lyle said after the game. "That showed me Billy had confidence in me; otherwise he never would have used me in a situation like that."

Billy Martin, within a game of his first pennant, seemed surprisingly tense in postgame interviews. He was short with reporters, as if waiting for someone to challenge him. "All year long one of you guys would ask, 'Is this the most important game of the year?' and for the first time this season, nobody bothered to ask it," he said, with acid in his voice. "Well, this was the biggest win of all."

A reporter asked Billy why he was able to get along with Dock Ellis when other managers seemed to have had problems with him. "Maybe other managers are prejudiced against blacks," Martin said, with a smile that meant: You figure out if that's a straight answer or a put-on. "He tells me I'm hurting his image as a troublemaker and he won't be able to go back to the ghetto."

Martin announced that Catfish Hunter would pitch the next game, taking a three-day rest instead of his usual four days. "Tomorrow is the day," he said. "The day after tomorrow will take care of itself. Right now we're one game away, and, fellows, it's time for my Scotch and soda," he said, concluding the interview.

Many were surprised that Martin did not pitch Ken Holtzman in the fourth, holding Catfish for the fifth if necessary. Among those surprised was Whitey Herzog. The next morning Whitey telephoned Billy and asked, "Are you really pitching Hunter?"

"Yep," Billy said.

After the way Catfish had returned to his old form in the first game, Billy was totally confident the pennant would be his by the end of the game. So were the rest of the Yankees. Kansas City won, 7–4. In the press-interview room after the game Martin stood next to the podium and watched while reporters directed questions at Hal McRae, a game star for the Royals. McRae said he thought the Royals were in the better position to win the fifth game because the Yankees would not have as much confidence in their pitcher as they had in Hunter.

Martin then took his turn in front of the microphones and announced his fifth game pitcher would be Ed Figueroa—"and I've got a lot of confidence in him."

"What about Holtzman?" a reporter asked.

"What about him?" Billy snapped back.

"Well, ahhh, why'd you pick Figueroa over Holtzman?"

"I think nineteen wins is a pretty good reason."

Martin saw one bright spot in the game. "We didn't win, but we had a pretty good night," he said. "We knocked out their superpitcher, Gura." Larry Gura had lasted only two innings, giving up six hits.

In the Yankee clubhouse players sat slumped in front of their lockers, speaking in whispers when they spoke at all. George Steinbrenner came in to cheer up the troops. While Martin was answering reporters' questions, Steinbrenner moved from locker to locker, giving pep talks. "C'mon now, you're come too far to do this," he said to Sandy Alomar, patting him on the head. "Get your chin up," he told Chris Chambliss. Catfish Hunter's locker was surrounded by newsmen. "I think my arm would have been a little stronger with another day's rest," Hunter admitted. "I didn't think I'd pitch until the fifth game, but he said pitch, so I pitch. When he says here's the ball, I'll take it."

Whatever was going to happen in the fifth game, the playoffs were not turning out to be the easy Yankee victory Martin and his players had expected. Martin had taken his best shot and lost with Hunter in the fourth game. Now he was going with the pitcher who had lost the second game and who always had trouble with Kansas City.

"I wish *I* had Holtzman," Herzog commented. "I'd sure use him."

Steinbrenner was worried about his team. He could not just sit back and watch them; he had to help. He decided to straighten out the Mickey Rivers problem. In the playoffs Rivers had been hitting and fielding poorly. And he had a "communications problem" with Martin. Steinbrenner invited Rivers into his office for a chat just before the final game. "He wants to know you care about him," the principal owner later explained. He told Mickey that as he goes, so goes the ballclub. The chat was short, the kind football coaches give at halftime. That night Rivers would collect four hits and score three runs.

Tough situations bring out Martin's most combative nature. When reporters filed onto the field to watch batting practice before the final game, they found a rope barring their approach to the batting cage. Reporters gather much of their feature material by talking with the players as they wait their turns at batting practice, and they didn't like a rope keeping them away. When Martin came to the dugout, Dick Young, sports editor of the *Daily News*, approached him and requested that the rope be taken down. Martin did not say the barrier was Steinbrenner's idea—he assumed responsibility for it himself and met the sportswriter's challenge. It was there to protect the reporters from the risk of foul balls, Martin explained. "I'll take the personal risk," Young said. "I've never seen a reporter hit by a foul ball in forty years. Billy, I'm telling you, it will cause hard feelings. We want to hear the chatter, talk to the guys."

"I like the rope," Martin said, provoking the feisty sportswriter. "I'd like to rope off the whole field."

"Why don't you tell the fans to go home, too?" Young shouted.

"I'm the boss here," Martin replied. "I don't tell you how to run your newspaper."

Furious, Young went back to the barrier and kicked it over. A security guard put it up again. Later, after reporters appealed to Yankee and league officials, the rope barrier was removed.

The final game of the 1976 American League championship series met the most ardent baseball fan's demands for drama. The Royals jumped off to a 2–0 lead in the first half of the first inning. Yankee fans groaned, fearing their hopes had been an illusion. Then the Yankees tied it with two runs in the bottom of the first. Kansas City again took the lead with a run in the second. The lead changed as the Yankees scored two in the third. Then they added two in the sixth for a 6–3 lead, and the crowd relaxed. The Yankees had battled back, and now, with a three-run advantage and only three innings left, New York had its long-awaited pennant. A scoreless seventh bolstered the hometown fans' confidence.

In the top of the eighth, with only six outs to go, George Brett faced relief pitcher Grant Jackson with two on—and hit a three-run, game-tying home run. The Yankee crowd deflated. The momentum had swung the other way now, and the Royals looked like winners. "He's got Tidrow and Lyle and he's gotta bring in Jackson ferchrissakes," a hefty fan complained in the men's room, ready to pin the blame on Martin for blowing the pennant. In the dugout Martin thought, an inning ago the pennant was so close, and now . . . But he heard noise around him. Instead of sitting in quiet depression, his players were cheering and yelling— they believed they could win.

The Yankees could not score in the bottom of the eighth. In the top of the ninth, two Royals were on with two out when Al Cowens was called out on a very close force play at second. If Herzog were Martin, the explosion would have been heard in midtown Manhattan. But Herzog is not Martin, and he reluctantly accepted the umpire's judgment.

Yankee fans were growing more restless and rambunctious. As the Royals took the field in the bottom of the ninth, garbage flew out of the stands toward right fielder Hal McRae. The umpires called time and the announcer requested, "Please refrain from throwing objects on the field." Kansas City relief pitcher Mark Littell took a few more warmup pitches. Chris Chambliss stood in the on-deck circle, swinging his bat and studying the pitcher.

Billy Martin was tense as a piano wire. The Yankees couldn't lose. *He* couldn't lose, not with this team, the team everyone had expected to win. He couldn't lose, and yet, he knew he might. He said a Hail Mary, something he had never before done during a baseball game. "Come on, Chris, you can do it." *Hail Mary full of grace the Lord is with thee. Blessed art thou among women and blessed is the fruit of thy womb Jesus. . . . Thank God it's Chambliss up there, a helluva player, a helluva clutch hitter.* "Get it going, Chris, you can hit this guy, goddammit!" *Holy Mary Mother of God pray for us sinners now and at the hour of our death amen.*

The field was cleared of debris, the crowd quieted and Chambliss stepped up to the plate. Littell knew what his first pitch would be. He would challenge with a fastball inside—that was a pitch Chambliss would either belt or miss entirely. He missed it last time around. Littell's fastball came in waist high, Chris's bat came around—a line-drive home run just over the fence in right field.

Echoes from a quarter of a century before, almost to the day: in the bottom of the ninth Bobby Thomson hits the "shot heard around the world," the home run that wins the pennant for the New York Giants, and New Yorkers, the ones who do not live in Brooklyn, go wild.

Chambliss leaped as the ball cleared the fence. In the dugout Martin leaped, and leaped again, "like a little kid I was so excited." The fans leaped—over the barriers and onto the field, by the thousands. As Chris reached second base, he saw it floating away in a sea of fans. He reached his hand out and touched it, then continued his epic journey around the bases, until he reached shortstop; and down he went, disappearing into the human swarm. He climbed back to his feet and headed for home, running desperately now as well as joyfully. Teammates and police battled through the mob to escort Chris home.

On the field people yelled their joy. In the neighborhood streets of the decaying South Bronx, people danced. In the bars of midtown Manhattan strangers cheered together.

The Yankees won the pennant! Chris Chambliss won the pennant! Billy Martin brought the pennant back to New York!

Television cameras have shown hundreds of winners' locker rooms after championship games in all sports. Always there is loud whooping, crowds of people milling about, champagne being drunk from bottles and poured over people's heads. Often emotion is performed for the cameras by players who know what is expected of them. In the Yankee clubhouse, though, the emotion was genuine, the joy explosive.

Billy Martin—Billy the Kid, the Dead End Kid, exiled from the Yankees and bounced around two leagues—drinking from a bottle of champagne, his hair wet with it, stood, between a small man named Abe Beame and a silver-haired gentleman named Cary Grant, television crews providing beatific light. "I've never been as excited as this," Billy choked. "Not even when I got that big hit in the fifty-three Series. It wasn't that passionate a scene."

"Billy," Mayor Beame said, "you really kept New York on top."

"Billy," Cary Grant said, "the Mayor called Chambliss's home run."

"Did he?" Martin replied. "That's really amazing." Putting his arm around the small mayor, Billy said to him, "I'm looking forward to doing this again next year."

"It must have been terrible when Brett hit that homer," Beame said.

"I was very depressed," Billy said, "but when the guys came off the field after that inning, they were really talking it up. We've got a great bunch. They don't quit."

Shouts and whoops kept erupting. Crowds surged back and forth—players, newsmen, television crews, Yankee officials. Reporters pushed near Chris Chambliss's locker as if it were a rush-hour subway train door, and Chris repeated his answers over and over. Thurman Munson grabbed a microphone out of a reporter's hand and parodied an interview with his manager. "Tell me, Billy, just what did you think when you saw the ball go over the wall?"

"Well, I thought it was a home run," Billy deadpanned, then broke up laughing. He grabbed Ed Figueroa and hugged him, yelling to all, "How do you like my Puerto Rican now?"

"What about those fans, Billy?"

"They weren't trying to hurt nobody, but they were going cra–zy!"

Billy Martin moved through the crowd. Like a 1950s teenager, he would rear back in mock surprise, palms up and shoulders jiggling, shout, "Heyyyy," then embrace a player or coach.

George Steinbrenner plowed his way through the mob to throw his arm around Billy's shoulder. Martin responded with his arm around George's waist, not bothering to fight for the superior arm position. "I'm proud of him," George said.

"I got to thank George, and Gabe," Martin said. "There was no backdooring. No one going behind my back to them.

"I wish Casey were here to see it," Billy said. "This was his pennant."

Outside the clubhouse door, in the mobbed corridor, players' wives jumped up and down, calling to their husbands to come out and share a joyous moment with them. Gretchen Martin waited for her husband in the Yankee offices. Billy sent an official from the clubhouse with a message where and when he would meet her, after the celebration in the clubhouse was over.

As the noise began to settle down, Billy was still steaming with sentiment and emotion. "It's like a mother watching her child get married," he said of his team. "Let the glory go to them. Seeing it come back to New York means the most to me." Then he shouted, "What are they going to say in Texas and Detroit and Minnesota now?"

Back in his office, Billy switched from champagne to Chivas Regal. He shook hands with reporters who offered their final congratulations before heading for their typewriters. He spotted a Cleveland reporter and said, "Hey, who's that guy on that late-night Cleveland show who's always riding me? I got a message for him—I want you to print it in your paper. Tell him to kiss my dago ass!"

Billy laughed with joy, the most joy he had ever known or would know again for a while.

Chapter 15
BACK ON THE PROVING GROUND

On Saturday, October 16, a sunny autumn morning, Billy Martin stood on the plastic grass of Cincinnati's Riverfront Stadium. Like an eager kid, he craned his neck to follow every hit of batting practice. Billy was back where he knew he belonged, in the World Series. Once again, he was on the final proving ground. As a player in the World Series, he had proved he was a winner. Now for the first time he would prove it as a manager.

A reporter asked Martin what he thought about the betting line establishing the Reds as favorites. "I don't care what Pete the Greek thinks," Martin said. "I never met a Greek who was a smart baseball player. All that talk about how great the Reds are and how great the National League is, that's not going to bother me. We used to beat them all easy in the Series when I played."

Now that he had led his Yankees back to the Series after they'd wandered in the wilderness for eleven years, Martin was confident he could lead them to the final victory. He would do it by managing the way he had all season—driving his players and controlling the game with aggressive, unpredictable strategy.

Martin's first unpredicted move of the '76 Series was to start his number five pitcher, Doyle Alexander, in the first game. Alexander had not pitched in three weeks. Catfish Hunter and Ed Figueroa needed more rest after the playoffs. But everyone thought, and Martin had hinted earlier, that the pitcher would either be Dock Ellis, who had last pitched on Tuesday, or Ken Holtzman, who had not been used in the playoffs. Holtzman had a 4–1 World Series record with the Oakland A's and was 8–3 lifetime against the Reds, including a no-hitter when he was a Chicago Cub.

"I've picked Alexander," Martin explained, "because he has a herky-jerky motion which could bother the Reds. I also like him here on artificial turf because he throws flyball outs and keeps the ball off the ground."

Joe Morgan, the third batter up for the Reds that afternoon, helped Alexander keep the ball off the ground—he hit it into the right-field stands. Something else went wrong for the Yankees before the first inning was over. Reds owner Bob Howsam protested to Commissioner Bowie Kuhn about the Yankee walkie-talkie scouts' being near a TV monitor in a radio booth. Howsam feared they might peek a look at the TV screen, read catcher Johnny Bench's signs to the pitcher, and use a code to relay the signs to Martin. He did not trust Martin, a fine sign-stealer in his day, not to take an extra edge. Kuhn telephoned orders to have the Yankee scouts removed from the radio booth. Before the inning was over, Billy came out of the dugout to confer with George Steinbrenner and Gabe Paul about the shutdown in communications. Paul then hustled over to Kuhn's box to argue.

On the field, things did not go well for Martin's nonelectronically guided players. The Yankees scored one run in the second; but twice, in the fifth and the seventh, the Yankee leadoff batter reached first only to be cut down by a double play. The sixth inning was the real breaker. With the Reds ahead 2–1, Mickey Rivers, successful on 43 of 50 base-stealing attempts in '76, reached first with one out. Martin gave the sign and Rivers ran. Bench threw to second, and the pride of the Yankees' running game was a clean out. Roy White then reached second on an error, and Thurman Munson lined a single to right—a hit that usually scores a runner from second. But scouting reports had warned Martin that the Reds' outfielders, unlike the Yankees', had strong arms. White did not challenge right fielder Ken Griffey's arm. He died on third, and with him the last Yankee hope of the game. The Reds scored one more in the sixth and two in the seventh for an easy 5–1 victory.

Questioned after the game about his anti-walkie-talkie ruling, Commissioner Kuhn said, "There was a dispute about the use of the walkie-talkies by the Yankees. I gave them permission, but then I found out they were being used in a way contrary to our agreement. I withdrew our permission." Asked if the Yankees were using the walkie-talkies for spying, Kuhn drew himself up and intoned, "I have no indications they were using them to steal signs. I will be asking penetrating questions."

Kuhn provided Billy with a focus for his anger during postgame interviews. "I didn't do anything different from what was requested by the commissioner's office," Martin said. "Anyone who says that, it's a false lie. There were no instructions where to use them."

A reporter asked if Martin weren't sticking his neck out by disputing the commissioner. "I'm telling the truth. Can they hang me for that?" Billy replied.

Will you request permission from Kuhn for walkie-talkies in Sunday's game? "No," Billy said. "His word's no good. I'm not going to ask him no more. I wouldn't ask him for permission if my heart was on fire."

Martin did not ask permission. Other Yankee officials did, and the commissioner of baseball granted it, provided

the Yankees kept their walkie-talkie scouts away from the
TV monitors.

Martin, like most American males, had spent much of
Sunday watching pro-football games on television in his
hotel room. Now, in the late afternoon, he stood with his
hands in his warmup jacket, watching practice. He complained to reporters about the weather. He complained
about having to start a World Series only two days after
finishing the playoffs. Nevertheless, Billy was in a cheerful
mood. He was in the World Series, rather than watching it
on television. And he was only one game down. That was
not enough, now that he had a day to cool down, to shake
his confidence in eventual victory. Billy pointed to a small
boy in a baseball uniform, half swallowed by a Yankee
warmup jacket, standing in shallow right field in front of
Yankee players, patiently waiting for a fly ball to come his
way. "That's my son, Billy Joe," Martin said, smiling. "He's
eleven, and quite an athlete for a kid his size."

Billy's cheerfulness faded quickly when he was asked
when Holtzman would pitch. "When I tell him to get up,"
the Yankee manager snapped, closing the subject.

The second game of the 1976 World Series was played on
a Sunday night, because there was more TV money if the
Series did not compete with afternoon pro football. Before
the game, 55,000 shivering fans were entertained by the
Ohio State marching band. Being a football band, they
were in mid-season form. And being a football band, they
needed a football field to play on, so they laid one down in
the outfield with white tape for yard markers. Then they
went through their intricate marching routines while playing Ohio State fight songs. The temperature was in the low
40s, on its way to 39 before the game ended.

Bowie Kuhn sat smiling in his box seat, wearing no over-
coat, attempting to convince everyone that it was a balmy
baseball evening. In the dugout Martin took his stance.

Hands in his back pockets, he alternately rocked on his heels and paced as he watched the game with the intensity of a Napoleon studying troop movements at Waterloo.

In the Cincinnati half of the second inning, the Reds' designated hitter, Danny Driessen, led off with a double. When George Foster scored him with a single, Martin reacted only with a shake of his head. After Thurman Munson caught Foster stealing, Bench hit a double. Martin looked to Munson for a sign that would tell him if Catfish was losing his stuff. Hunter threw one ball to César Geronimo, and Billy came trotting out to the mound for a conference. After trotting back to the dugout, he watched Geronimo walk, Davey Concepcion single in Bench, Concepcion steal second, Pete Rose walk, and Geronimo score on Ken Griffey's fly to center.

All the while, Martin remained calm. He shifted his feet, hugged himself against the cold and clenched his jaw. He stood apart from his players, speaking only an occasional word with pitching coach Bob Lemon. Munson finally ended the inning with a fine catch of a difficult pop foul. Martin gave Munson a pat on the butt as he came in, but did not speak with him or with Catfish. For Martin, the World Series was too intense and personal an experience for conversation—and the players seemed to know better than to engage their manager in chatter. The only players who sat anywhere near Martin while the Yankees batted were Munson and Graig Nettles.

When the Reds batted, coach Gene Michael worked the walkie-talkie and Yogi Berra waved the outfielders around. Martin did not pay much attention to the electronic scouting now that the Yankees had won their point.

In the Yankee fourth, with New York down 3–0, Martin huddled on the bench against the cold. Munson's infield single failed to draw Billy to his feet. Then, with one out, Chambliss singled and Nettles singled, scoring the Yankees' first run. Martin bounced up, clapped his hands, barked encouragement and popped gum into his mouth. The rally died with only the one run.

Martin became animated again in the Yankee sixth. With two on and one out, Billy's least-favorite player, Elliott Maddox, got shouts of encouragement at the plate from his least-favorite manager. Maddox hit into a double play. Martin looked at his feet, then headed for the tunnel to the locker room to warm himself at a gas heater.

The Yankee tying rally finally came, in the seventh. After Willie Randolph singled, Martin went through an elaborate series of signals. Randolph broke with the pitch and scored on Fred Stanley's double. The dugout warmed with cheers and applause. Martin smiled and Randolph received the second butt-pat from the Yankee manager. Stanley scored the tying run, and Martin's first World Series victory as a manager now seemed closer. When Morgan came to bat in the Cincinnati half of the seventh, Martin's fighting instinct surfaced. With his lips curled back, he shouted a steady stream of insults in his hoarse voice.

In the bottom of the ninth, the score was still tied 3–3. The Yankees would have to win in extra innings—and they would. They'd already proved they had the stuff of champions, Yankee pride, by coming back from three runs down, and Catfish looked strong. Billy Martin was moving, pacing, clapping, and shouting encouragement. The coaches near Martin, Elston Howard and Yogi Berra, echoed him. The rest of the bench joined in, cheering for Catfish and the Yankee defense. One out. Two outs. Then Ken Griffey was on second on Stanley's wild throw to first.

The next move was obvious. It could have been signaled from the dugout—but Martin had to be involved. He walked out to confer with Catfish and to tell him to walk Morgan and pitch to Tony Pérez. Billy returned to the dugout. It was cold there, colder than it ever had been.

Perez hit a line drive to left, driving in the winning run. Martin's head went down. He said nothing to anybody. He did not wait for his team to come off the field. As Griffey stepped on home plate, Billy walked into the ramp leading to the clubhouse, his team silently trailing behind him.

Ten minutes later, in the press-interview room, Martin faced a mob of sports reporters. He was asked if he had thought of removing Hunter in the second inning. During the season he had answered such routine questions without hesitation. Now he was too angry. "I never mention that after a ballgame's over. It's not important," he said. The weather was a target for some of his anger. "It's ridiculous—football weather," he complained. "It was miserable out there. Yogi has frostbite."

Then Billy offered his explanation for the fact that the Reds were two games up. "You have to have a little luck to win," he said, "and we haven't been getting it. They hit bloopers and they fall in. We hit line drives and they catch them."

"Which hits would you describe as bloopers, Billy?" asked a reporter who did not cover the Yankees on a regular basis.

"Weren't you at the game?" Martin shot back.

"Yeah, but they didn't look like blooper hits to me."

"Come to batting practice on Monday and I'll show you what a blooper is," Martin said, his temper approaching critical mass.

A few reporters followed Martin from the interview room to the visiting manager's office off the locker room, heard him repeat "bloopers" and "luck" a few times, and quickly left. Billy Joe Martin, playing in the locker room, stayed out of his daddy's office.

On Monday at four o'clock, the scheduled time for a Yankee off-day practice session, a chill wind was blowing at Yankee Stadium. Martin sat in his office, fielding questions. He spoke again of luck and of bloopers. If the reporter who asked the original blooper question was there, he didn't identify himself. Asked if he would describe the Reds as "awesome," Martin reacted sharply. "The only awesome team I ever saw were the Yankees of the 1950s." Billy put on a baseball shirt for a TV interview in the clubhouse, but he never did make it out to the field to join his players. Before five o'clock, all the players drifted in, shivering and complaining of the cold.

On Tuesday evening Mickey Rivers stirred the Yankees' hopes in the first inning by reaching first on a bunt and a throwing error by the pitcher. Seeing Rivers at first made George Steinbrenner feel better. Earlier that day he had had Rivers in for another pep talk. It had worked in the playoffs. Tonight it did not work as well—Rivers was picked off first. Munson singled and Martin thought this might be the right time to create some excitement to ignite his team. He charged out to first base, placed his jaw within an inch of the umpire's nose and explained that Reds pitcher Pat Zachry was using a balk motion in throwing to first. Neither the first-base umpire nor the home-plate umpire agreed. And the Yankees failed to score.

In the second inning a fidgeting Martin watched Driessen reach first on a poor throw by Randolph. Driessen stole second as Munson missed the handle pulling the ball out of his glove. Foster scored Driessen with a ground-rule double. Bench beat out an infield hit. Geronimo hit a double-play ball but beat the throw to first as Foster scored. Munson knew Geronimo would be stealing and called for a pitchout, and still couldn't catch him at second. When Concepcion singled to left, Geronimo scored. Again the Yankees were behind 3–0, and this time there was to be no dramatic New York comeback.

While Sparky Anderson sat in his dugout, chatting with his coaches or with Johnny Bench, Martin paced. Or he leaned against the dugout wall near the exit to the clubhouse. Or he propped his foot on the dugout step and stared out at the game. He watched Mickey Rivers hesitate coming in on a fly ball, turning an out into a hit. In the seventh he watched in disbelief as Jim Mason hit a home run to make the score 4–2. Mason, playing because Fred Stanely had been removed for a pinch hitter, came back into the dugout gleeful. He received congratulations from his excited teammates and a handshake from his manager. Then Billy resumed his glum isolation, as if he sensed what was to come. The next two Yankees got on base. Then, with one out, Munson lined a shot up the first-base line, where it was grabbed by Pérez, who then threw to second to double up Rivers.

The Reds scored two more in the eighth, winning 6–2. The game had kept most Yankee fans on the seat of their pants. Again, Martin did not wait for his players. He was quickly out of the dugout and into the clubhouse. When he appeared in the interview room, he said, "Every time we hit the ball hard, it seems to go right at someone. . . . Their bloopers have fallen in. . . . They only hit three balls hard tonight for hits."

Martin announced that Ed Figueroa would pitch the fourth game and Holtzman the fifth. "Holtzman? How do you spell that?" a voice called out from the back of the room. Billy Martin did not think that was funny. The tightness came into his voice as he replied, "If you can't spell, you don't belong in this room."

Back in the clubhouse, Martin was ready to explode. He marched around asking, "Who's that guy who asked how to spell Holtzman? I'd like to see him . . . in private. Tell him to come in my office. I'll spell it on his forehead." One reporter said, "Oh, he wasn't a reporter. They threw him out of the room after you left—he didn't have press credentials."

Having let off some steam, Martin relaxed a little and sat down behind his desk in his office. He spoke of the problems of the scheduling, ducked a question about Elliott Maddox, and again explained that "the Reds are real good, but they're not awesome. You can't take nothing away from them. But I haven't seen this super power. I've seen bloopers."

Encouraged by reporters, he reminisced about the team that was "awesome"—the '50 Yankees. He bragged that he was on six consecutive pennant winners. He was in the Army, "fighting communism" in 1954 when Cleveland interrupted the Yankee string. "And you're still fighting Reds, huh, Billy?" a reporter remarked. Martin laughed, quickly adding, "I don't know what I'm laughing for. It ain't that funny."

He started talking about his Army days. He did not want to leave his office, not just yet while he had a sympathetic audience. "I got a good-conduct medal, too," he said, flashing a grin at one reporter. "Shove that up your ass, Gerry."

The real subject of the hour—losing three in a row—had to come up again. How does it feel, Billy? "I'd rather have you punch me three times in the stomach and have a chance to retaliate than be beaten like this," he said.

The punches reminded him of something else. "You know, I wish I knew that guy wasn't a reporter. I'd have come down off that podium and given him a real asskicking," Martin said, forgetting he was ready to give a real asskicking *before* he found out the guy wasn't a reporter. But now, among more sympathetic reporters, he explained that he knew the press had to bait him occasionally, just to get something to write, and that was why he wouldn't beat up a reporter.

"When you lose, it's a bitter pill to swallow," Martin went on. "Then, having to go in and answer questions, that's tough—without having a wiseass. . . . The more I think about it, the madder I get. It would have been a pleasure to kick the hell out of him."

Then Martin replayed the scene. He wouldn't throw the first punch, he said—he never did that. No, Martin explained, he'd walk up to the guy, get real close, then say something like, "You're a piece of shit." As soon as the guy made a motion with his arm, Martin would punch his lights out.

"We're with you, Billy," a reporter said. "Let's all go get that guy."

Billy was feeling better now. He smiled as he remembered a fight he had in a Minnesota bar, when some guy bet his friend $20 that he could lick Billy Martin. The guy surprised Martin, slugging him as he sat on a barstool. Martin climbed off the floor and knocked the gambler unconscious.

"Aw, but fighting's a pain in the ass," Martin said, not convincing anyone he meant it. "I got a boy, eleven years old. When he hears all that stuff about his daddy being in fights, I tell him if I'd been six-five, I'd never have been in a fight."

His boy, carefully avoiding the clubhouse tonight, was busy building pyramids of plastic glasses in the "hospitality room" down the hall, amid Yankee guests and drinking reporters.

For Yankee fans the best part of the fourth game, delayed one day by rain, came before the game started. As a cold wind swirled through the Stadium, blowing peanut shells on the heads of the patrons. A high-school marching band entertained. When they concluded their last number, a dozen young majorettes turned their backs to the crowd, bent over, lifted their skirts, and, with a letter on each pair of panties, mooned out GO YANKEES.

The Yankees tried, but the Reds were awesome. Behind Munson's four-for-four hitting, New York scored one in the first and one in the fifth. The Reds, with Johnny Bench hitting two home runs, scored three in the fourth and four in the ninth. It was over. Including their playoff sweep over the Philadelphia Phillies, the Reds had won seven straight postseason games. They had outscored the Yankees 22–8.

They had stolen 7 bases in 11 attempts, while the Yankees had managed only 1 stolen base in 3 attempts.

This time, Martin did not wait for the end before heading for the clubhouse. Cincinnati was only leading 3–2 in the top of the ninth, and theoretically the Yankees could have won—but they did not look like a winning team at that point. Everyone in the stands knew it. The players knew it. Even Billy Martin, always sure of victory against all odds, knew it. Tony Pérez walked and took second on a wild pitch. Then Driessen hit a foul ball into the Yankee dugout. Martin, who had spent much of the game yelling at plate umpire Bill Deegan, picked up the ball and threw it at Deegan. Just as quickly, first-base umpire Bruce Froemming gave Martin the heave, and out of the dugout stormed the Yankee manager, all his pent-up frustrations detonating.

Martin leaped and shouted, seeming no more in control of himself than a child in a tantrum. The umpires had one major fear: 56,000 happy Yankee fans had mobbed the field a week before, in the ninth inning of the last game of the playoffs. What might 56,000 frustrated Yankee fans do in the ninth inning of a losing World Series, given a spark? Riot? While Froemming held his ground against the screaming manager, the other umpires rushed over, restrained Martin, and told him to get out fast.

Billy left, kicking the bat rack as he went. Yogi Berra, twice a World Series manager, took over and watched the Reds score four more runs.

Thurman Munson was sent to the interview room to represent Martin. Reporters then went to Martin's office. He was not there. He was not in the players' area of the clubhouse. As the Yankess slumped dejectedly in front of their lockers, George Steinbrenner represented Yankee authority in the clubhouse. He spoke about how it had been a great year despite the loss, and moved from locker to locker telling the players they had nothing to be ashamed of. "There's five hundred fifty major-league ballplayers sitting at home who weren't in this Series," he said. "We'll be back." The Yankee manager still did not appear.

Half an hour after the game, Martin, looking drained and red-eyed, stood at the door of the trainer's room, which was off limits to the press. "I'm sorry, gentlemen," he said in a subdued voice to the reporters crowding around the doorway. "I was just too upset." Billy held a plastic glass of Scotch in his hand. A week ago it had been champagne. He looked skinny—he said that he had lost twenty pounds during the season and now weighed 154.

Martin explained that he had no quarrel with the ejection call, since ejection is automatic when you throw something from the dugout. He said he threw the baseball at Deegan because three times during the game, while Deegan was tossing used baseballs into the dugout, the umpire had thrown the baseballs at Martin. The umpire was throwing baseballs at Billy Martin, in front of 56,000 fans and reporters, and nobody else had noticed it?

"Ah, Billy, why did Deegan throw baseballs at you?"

"I was on him a lot," Martin said. "He called a brutal game. During the regular season, I'd have been thrown out by the third inning."

A reporter asked about the final scene, when it looked as if the umpires were having to restrain him. "I should have popped one of them for grabbing ahold of me," Martin said. "They're not supposed to do that."

About the Reds, Billy? "I hope the Reds are there next year, because next year we'll win in four straight and we'll see how they like it. I want to show people that this was a fluke."

Just how good are the Reds, Billy? "The Reds are great, but not awesome. Every time we had opportunities we hit a line drive at someone—all through the Series. . . . Bloopers. . . ."

Billy, have you been crying? "Yes," he said. "I'm not ashamed of it. I'm an emotional guy. . . . It hurts my pride, my ego I guess, to lose like this."

It had happened before. After the 1955 World Series, when the Dodgers defeated the Yankees, Martin had hid in the trainer's room and wept. "It isn't right for a man like Casey to lose," he had told Mickey Mantle.

In 1976, twenty-one years later, Martin again wept for the Yankees and their manager.

Chapter 16
MORE CHALLENGES FOR THE GUNFIGHTER

At forty-nine, Billy Martin has achieved much against heavy odds. He battled up from poverty, from an insecure, fatherless childhood. Pushing his good but not extraordinary athletic abilities to their limits, he made himself into one of the most valuable players on the great Yankee teams of the 1950s. When his playing days ended in obscurity, he carved out a new baseball career for himself. He succeeded as a coach and then as a manager. And he did it on his own implacable terms. On the field, he turned losing teams into winners. In the executive suites, he lost. By refusing to become a good company man, he precipitated his own firings. Then he made his return to the Yankees into a triumph, bringing the American League pennant back to New York.

In his first year of a three-year, $100,000-plus-per-year contract, Martin entered the 1977 season as a champion. His success might have been enough to bank another person's inner fires—but not Billy Martin's. For Billy, there were more challenges that had to be met and overcome.

He had to win the pennant again, especially since the off-season trades and free-agent signings greatly strengthened the Yankees, on paper at least. Next he had to win the World Series to avenge the personal insult of having been swept in four games. And in order to do either he had to control his temper and rebelliousness enough to retain his job.

If Martin could lead his team to a second consecutive pennant, it would help dispel the most common knock against him—that he is a "short-term manager." He can quickly turn a team into a winner by force of his personality and his intensity, his critics say, but in the long run that intensity cannot be sustained. Players who respond to the extremes of his anger and his praise eventually become disillusioned with his leadership. When a team of his suffers a prolonged slump, as did the 1973 Tigers and the 1975 Rangers, Martin's uncontrolled anger produces turmoil and dissension. He does not have the patience to wait out the bad times. Early in the 1977 season the critics' theories were being put to the test as the Yankees dropped into the division cellar by losing 8 of their first 10 games, and Martin strained to maintain his composure. Even after the Yankees began winning, Martin remained constantly near the boiling point. His relationships with his players, particularly newly acquired superstar Reggie Jackson, and with his boss George Steinbrenner deteriorated.

In 1976 his dealings with George Steinbrenner were not smooth but were better than Martin's past relationships with his bosses. At the end of the '76 season and through the off-season, Steinbrenner moved more and more toward center stage. He gave private pep talks to Mickey Rivers during the playoffs and the World Series. He visited the clubhouse and chatted with the players. After the season, he personally wooed and won free agent Reggie Jackson, and enjoyed the publicity he received for it. Martin did not play a role in the Jackson signing, and he worried that Reggie and George would continue their close relationship and bypass the Yankee manager. "Backdooring"—direct dealings between the front office and players—is a cardinal sin in the Martin book of managing.

During spring training, tension began to build between Martin and Steinbrenner, as the manager resisted the owner's increasing involvement in the operations of the team. After a loss to the Mets late in March, Steinbrenner charged into the clubhouse and had a shouting match with the manager in front of the players. It ended with Martin's daring Steinbrenner to fire him. The two supposedly patched up their disagreements over breakfast the next day, but the Yankees' shakey early-season performance caused strains to reappear. In May, Martin publicly blasted his front office for failing to provide him with a third catcher—and Steinbrenner just as publicly fined Martin $2500, and began to mutter about hiring another manager.

On June 18, while the Yankees were being knocked out of first place by the Red Sox, Martin yanked Jackson in the middle of an inning for lack of hustle on a defensive play. When Jackson yelled at Martin in the dugout, Martin tried to punch him out and had to be restrained. The next day Martin failed to show up at a meeting with Gabe Paul and Steinbrenner to discuss the incident. Steinbrenner almost made up his mind to fire Martin, but a series of meetings with Martin, Jackson and the other players convinced Steinbrenner not to take the final step. Since rumors were flying about Martin's impending dismissal, Steinbrenner made the unusual move of appearing on national television to announce that Martin would not be fired—yet.

For long-term success with the Yankees, Martin will have to accept the frustrations of being number two. His mentor, Casey Stengel, accommodated himself to General Manager George Weiss and settled into a long tenure as Yankee manager. And long tenure is an appealing prospect for Martin. In the spring of '77 the Yankees looked to be very strong for years to come, not only because of their talent but also because their farm system had been revitalized by infusions of money.

Whatever happens on the 1977 Yankees, it will be difficult for Billy the Kid to approach Stengel's twelve-year hold on the Yankee managership. And what will likely prevent it will be those qualities that won him the job in the first place. Billy's independence, his fiery temperament, and his "us-against-them" view of the world have been essential to his success since his days as a sandlot player.

In many ways, Billy Martin is the classic American hero. He is the driven scrapper, willing to take on any opponent, no matter how big; willing to undertake any challenge, no matter how difficult. We admire people who battle successfully against overwhelming odds. We respect those who are more driven to succeed than the rest of us, more willing to go it alone. And we even look up to those more ruthless than we are in their push toward success. We are impressed by the way they can act with such enormous self-confidence, such bravado, even while we realize that it often stems from a deeper insecurity than the rest of us feel. Other countries' heroes may assume the mantle of leadership reluctantly. Ours thrust themselves toward it. The driven, hot-tempered, egotistical General George S. Patton stirs us more than does the more modest, balanced, and temperate General George Marshall.

Billy Martin is out of the Patton mold. His excesses are what excite us. We license the underdog to overreach, to exceed proprietry: Billy Martin has been the underdog most of his life. We applaud the fellow at the short end of the stick, even when he is a graceless winner and a poor loser. Our perception changes, however, when the hero is not the underdog. General Patton defying the Pentagon is much more appealing than General Patton slapping a private, though the two actions stem from the same intemperate character. Martin's insults to marginal players and rookie umpires do not evoke the same response in us as his blasts at Commissioner Kuhn.

Martin is intelligent enough to try to learn from his mistakes. He will try to make the effort to get along with his front office. He will attempt to achieve better rapport with his players and to remain calm in the crisis of a losing streak.

It will not be easy for him, for he is a man not at peace with himself or the world. And even the success that he is driven toward cannot confer that peace. The shifting fault lines of his psyche will continue to cause quakes around him. Some clashes with authority are inevitable, as are intemperate remarks, feuds, and fist fights—and more victories, before some final defeat.

"I can't change now," he has said. "I guess it's like being a gunfighter. Once you start, you do it for life—until somebody comes along and shoots you down."